THE SLUMBER OF APOLLO

THE SLUMBER OF APOLLO

REFLECTIONS ON RECENT ART,
LITERATURE, LANGUAGE, AND THE
INDIVIDUAL CONSCIOUSNESS

JOHN HOLLOWAY

Fellow of Queens' College, Cambridge and
Emeritus Professor of Modern English

CAMBRIDGE UNIVERSITY PRESS

Cambridge
London   New York   New Rochelle
Melbourne   Sydney

Published by the Press Syndicate of the University of Cambridge
The Pitt Building, Trumpington Street, Cambridge CB2 1RP
32 East 57th Street, New York, NY 10022, USA
296 Beaconsfield Parade, Middle Park, Melbourne 3206, Australia

BD 431
. H 66

First published 1983

Printed in Great Britain by
the University Press, Cambridge

Library of Congress catalogue card number: 83–14279

British Library cataloguing in publication data
Holloway, John
The slumber of Apollo: reflections on recent
art, literature, language, and the individual
consciousness.
1. Arts, European   2. Arts, Modern – Europe
I. Title
700'.94   NX542
ISBN 0 521 24804 3

UP

To my wife

CONTENTS

ILLUSTRATIONS

PREFACE

Some of the chapters in this book appeared first as the 'Virginia Lectures' given in the University of Charlottesville in 1979, but since then revised for publication. I should like to express gratitude to the University of Virginia, and its Committee for Comparative Study of Individual and Society, for inviting me to deliver those lectures, and more particularly to all those at Charlottesville from whose hospitality and kindness I benefited so much during my stay. I am also indebted to Andrew Brown and to Frank Kermode for helpful discussion and advice. Throughout, italics in quotations are added by the writer, to elucidate the point being made in the present discussion.

1   Piero della Francesca, *The Nativity* (detail)

2   Piero della Francesca, *The Death of Adam*, detail: face of Eve

3   Rembrandt, *Margaretha de Geer*

4   Koninck, *Landscape with Huts at Amsterdam*

5   Rufino Tamayo, *Man Singing*

6   Jean Dubuffet, *Woman Chanting*

7 Kasimir Malevich, *Scissors Grinder*

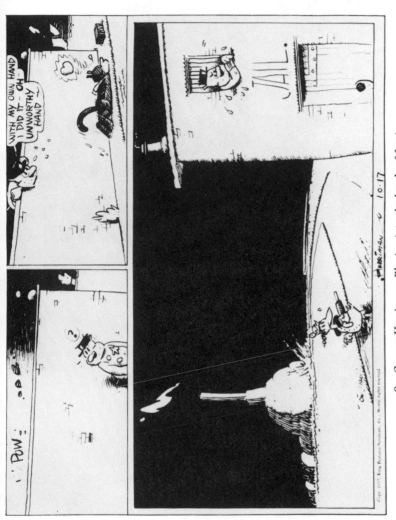

8 George Herriman, *Playing into the hands of fate!*

9   Russell Drysdale, *The Puckamanni*

10 Willem de Kooning, *Woman, I*

TERRIBLE RESULT OF THE HIGHER EDUCATION OF WOMEN!

INTRODUCTION

THIS BOOK has been written, not in the conviction, but to review the possibility, that the present time and the recent past have seen a certain major change in what makes up our lives and our ideals about life. That possibility is of a large but almost entirely unnoticed, or untraced, shift with regard to the consciousness and mental life of the individual. In brief, it seems that the shift may have been from mental life and consciousness, to describe which would naturally bring in terms like 'large', 'comprehending', 'thoughtful', 'contemplation' and the like, towards a consciousness and mental life more limited (though in its own way, perhaps intense sometimes), or more relaxed and unambitious, or more concerned with practicalities – including, in particular, the 'handling' of others, and those ranges of experience where personal life is absorbed, to a greater or lesser degree, in collective life. The former qualities I have thought of, following Nietzsche, as for the sake of brevity falling under the term 'Apollonian'. Hence the title of this book.

Certain points require to be cleared up, in advance of undertaking this perhaps excessively wide-ranging and so exploratory discussion. Of course, the people – the children – who worked underground, two hundred years ago, in the mines of the North of England (and many other places), probably enjoyed little by way of expansiveness of mental life and consciousness. The question is not of what conditions of life obtained universally, but of what used to be seen, and what on the other hand has perhaps been coming to be seen, as a conception of how life could be lived and of how it was best, or at the least adequately lived. Of course also, many have indeed realized, largely or partly, whatever has been the ideal of life that they have subscribed to. The purpose of the discussion is not to pass judgement, in some definitive way, upon the goodness or badness of how our world may have changed over the past hundred or hundred and fifty years. It is simply to explore a certain wide-ranging though somewhat elusive possibility: to consider where it seems to show, and also to review the writing of certain literary authors who may have been partly conscious of it and have reflected it in their work.

Because what is at issue is the matter of some pervasive and all-embracing change, I have tried to, as it were, 'spread my net' widely and to enter fields that I have found interesting and suggestive, even when I have had to enter them as an amateur. The risks are obvious, but what are our risks, collectively speaking, if no one ever makes such an attempt, unless he is a universal polymath? Thus the first five chapters of the book pursue its underlying theme in the contexts, respectively, of serious visual art; of certain aspects of comic art; of political writing and especially oratory; of slang, colloquialisms and 'jargon' as they appear in English; and of certain developments in the study of the individual personality by psychologists. In each case, those topics are followed out over a period of the past hundred years or so.

The three closing chapters of the book are more concerned with literature. Of these, the first is about the way that the character of 'large' mind, of capacious consciousness, was an explicitly formulated ideal for a number of nineteenth-century authors, and how that ideal seems to have been modified, and to an extent, deliberately set aside, in the work of Thomas Hardy. The second reviews the poetry of Gary Snyder, the poet of our own time who has so emphatically declared that the conditions of modern life do indeed foster a restricted and coarsened consciousness, and has striven so hard to re-establish an older integration with the natural environment, and the larger, more delicate awareness that, in his view, went with it. The third of these chapters, and the last in the book, considers three major novels (and also, briefly, the work of a poet) which might be said to create 'fables for our time' of some pervasive, barely recognized but all-transforming change from the larger consciousness, to something smaller and slighter. In other words, it is as if the authors of those works were more or less conscious of the sort of transition that this present book envisages; though as writers of fiction they saw such matters in terms of the group of characters who interacted in their novels, and saw them dramatically rather than discursively.

I ought to say plainly, that insofar as the suggestions and speculations of this book are valid, they do not relate only to ideas and ideals (whether implicit or not) of our own time and of an earlier time. They must relate also to experience and reality, to how men and women tend to live and, more important perhaps, what potential and limit for life they are likely to have in them. Also, if there is truth in the idea that some pervasive change may have been coming over human experience – or maybe one should say European, or Western European, or Anglo-Saxon experience – we need not think that that is for the first time. We believe already that such wide-ranging changes of consciousness have not uncommonly occurred, say at the close of major periods of history. For myself, I incline to the view that they are perhaps less dramatically and spectacularly placed over time than that. Quite possibly they are going on in all periods, they overlap, they do not come one at a time. Only, their rhythms of arrival are too slow-moving for them to form part of anyone's direct experience; or rather, if they do that, one thinks of them as part of the difference between being young, and being old, oneself, rather than between living in a past time, and in the present time. Consequently they are to be detected only by reflection, exploration, and what might be termed 'chancing one's arm' a little, as to one's findings; and I have written in that spirit.

I   PERSONALITIES AND PANORAMAS

L ET US ·GO BACK five hundred years, and consider three individual figures in paintings by Piero della Francesca. The first is that of the youthful angel playing a stringed instrument and perhaps singing *sotto voce*, in Piero's *Nativity* (National Gallery, London). The figure stands firmly upright, the right foot boldly advanced, the left planted behind it crosswise. There is the confidence and dignity of (one may infer) a performer who in a quite literal sense is inspired. The arms and shoulders speak with quiet eloquence of the bulk and weight of the instrument, of the gentle tension on the wrists and hands as they play. But these motor energies in the work seem to be merely a painter's way of stressing something else: the musician's eyes, their gaze lost in the distance; his tilted head as he listens in rapture to the heavenly harmonies made by himself and his angelic co-partners; and the expression of his whole face, deeply, blissfully absorbed. He is lost in profound emotion, lost in thought.

In the Central Italian town of Borgo San Sepolcro, Piero's *Resurrection* shows the figure of Christ in the actual moment of stepping from the tomb. The left foot, poised to take the weight of the body at the next step, the left hand holding up Christ's robe, the right arm and fingers on the staff, relaxed for a moment before they too take weight, all fill the picture once more with motor energies – but they draw the spectator into responses about masses and incipient move-ments, only to make still more profound the transition into the contemplation of Christ's consciousness that is demanded of us by his countenance. 'He seems to be part of the dream... of the sleeping soldiers; and has Himself the doomed and distant gaze of a somnambulist.' Those words about this picture are by Kenneth Clark.[1] It is an extraordinary

5

face, one that fills us with a sense of vast receding planes of consciousness as we gaze. Compassion or hurt, comprehension or bewilderment, incomparable authority and dignity or the mere frailty and barely conscious awareness of one but newly awakened from sleep – it is a face which leaves us, as it seems itself, 'lost in thought'. 'We see not the ballance...we are in a Mist', Keats wrote about the manifold depths of human consciousness.[2] Bernard Berenson's essay on *Piero della Francesca, or the Ineloquent in Art* has some words which especially fit this profound and enigmatical countenance. 'I am tempted to conclude that in the long run the most satisfying creations...remain ineloquent...[they have] no urgent communication to make...if they express anything it is character, essence, rather than momentary feelings or purpose. They manifest potentiality rather than actuality...Art...has been so overexpressive in recent decades.'[3]

For ourselves, it is hard to comprehend the idea of resurrection, and only too easy to comprehend that of death. But in his fresco *The Death of Adam* (Arezzo), Piero reminds the beholder of how this would not have been so for Eve. No one had ever seen a man die before; and Piero's Eve, in posture as well as in countenance, and just like his Christ, is lost in bewilderment, lost in thought. In Berenson's word, she is 'ineloquent' with depths of potentiality, of character – those that belong to great age. And when, in his cartoon *Hasta la Muerta* ('until death...') Goya produces a savage, ferret-like old woman resembling Piero's Eve enough to be a dreadful caricature of her, a senile but galvanized old harpy expressive, if any figure ever was, not of depth and potentiality but of narrow, bitter actuality, Goya then starts from something of the same underlying conception about human consciousness, and about the individual, but he deliberately shows, with horror, its debasement and its bestialization.

'Lost in thought'...if we come nearly two hundred years forward in time, and think for a moment about some of the portraits of Rembrandt, like the *Self-Portrait aged 63*, or the ravaged but determined and intensely humane *Margaretha de Geer* (both of these are in the National Gallery in London), we see another painter whose figures can be 'ineloquent' with profundity of personality and so of consciousness. Rembrandt's sitters make a clear contrast with, say, the portraits of a contemporary like Frans Hals. Hals's effervescent extroverts, who look as if they can just hold back their pointless chatter for long enough to let the artist rush off a quick sketch and retreat to the quiet of his studio, bring out by contrast what Rembrandt achieves. Margaretha de Geer's dazzling white cuff and ruffs, and so the whole tonality of that painting, are not the solution of formal problems alone: formal considerations focus into a silent invitation to us to contemplate what ruff and cuff throw into prominence: the face and the hands, expressive (though with restraint and dignity) of a whole human life – luminous epitomes of character and individuality.

But there is another kind of Dutch painting, in the seventeenth century, that calls for our attention. It does so because it suggests a possible answer to the question of what such absorbed, meditative, intensely engrossed countenances can be engrossed *with*. It is only a possibility: but a suggestive one. Perhaps there is a clue in Rembrandt's *David Harping before Saul* (Maritshuis, The Hague, about 1657). Saul, again, is 'lost in thought'; and so is the young David – a limited, striving version of Piero's effortless angel, a youth all absorption and dedication. But Browning, in his poem on the same subject, has David's playing link Saul's face, as he listens, to gazing at a seascape or a landscape – a 'sad level gaze o'er the ocean'; and it is not fanciful to suggest that seventeenth-century Dutch landscape offers a possible answer to our question. In saying this I am not thinking of the Dutch mountain scenes of the period; based, necessarily, on travel or on imagination. These seem heavy with wild, melodramatic feeling; they are closed in and self-sealing: Berenson's 'over-expressive' painting claustrophobically intensified. But when the Dutch depict their own vast flat landscape, all is otherwise. The swirlingly curvacious designs to which mountain scenes lend themselves are replaced by an austere and spacious discipline of gridded verticals and horizontals, provided by towers and spires on the one hand, and above all by water on the other. The endless expanse and endless detail of these great panoramas – I have in mind works by Koninck, Ruisdael, Hobbema and others – are based upon powerfully organized formal qualities. But among the endless offers of thought, among which they invite the spectator to lose himself, one, at least to a literary mind, is unquestionably the invitation to meditate and contemplate the question, *What is it like as Life* inside the spacious world of the painting? Both by literary means, and formally, the paintings of this school over and again invite us to meditate our way deep into the life-patterns of the picture. Even the cloudscapes powerfully contribute: cover them, and a giant landscape shrivels to a garden patch.

Some of the other paintings of this School extend a like invitation in other terms. Koninck's *Entrance to a Forest* (M. H. de Young Memorial Museum, California), Ruisdael's *Forest Entrance* (Vienna), Hobbema's *Road into a Forest* (Rotterdam), are examples of a conventionally established genre using the motif of the bosky track or pathway to draw the spectator into the picture world. But the most characteristic form is the great flat-land panorama, like Koninck's *Landscape with Huts at Amsterdam*. It anticipates, as it far outdistances, Dyer's early eighteenth-century poem, 'Grongar Hill':

> No clouds, no vapours intervene,
> But the gay, the open scene
> Does the face of Nature show,
> In all the hues of heaven's bow!
> And, spreading to embrace the light,
> Spreads around beneath the sight...

Koninck's *Huts at Amsterdam* is a panorama of ships, lakes, cities, fields and forests, all in glittering light or vast sombre shadow, all with endless detail of the fullness of life.

There is an application, or analogy, for all this in literature: one that was noticed by George Eliot. Suppose we were to ask where we might find profound portraiture of the deepest levels of thought and feeling in the individual, and at the same time a great panorama, both rural and urban, of social life. Obviously, we could scarcely expect to find these combined in any one painting. It would have to be both a portrait, and a landscape, all in one: though I must mention, in Chapter VII, certain paintings that in fact are of this kind. That is exactly what we do find, however, in one great literary achievement of modern times: the nineteenth-century novel. In *Le Père Goriot*, in *Madame Bovary*, in *Dead Souls* or *Anna Karenina*, in *Middlemarch* or *The Mayor of Casterbridge*, there before the reader lie just those two things: profound study of individual consciousness, both thought and feeling; and along with that, a sense of all-embracing, spacious, all-comprehended social and topographical order. The spatial order of the great Dutch landscapes is replaced by a temporal order and a causal order, at once synchronic and diachronic, of social interaction and of that perhaps greatest of nineteenth-century inventions, History.

Hence my title and its reference to Apollo. Nietzsche, in *The Birth of Tragedy*, took the god Apollo as symbol for a significant combination of qualities. He thought of Apollo as divine patron of the arts; of poetry; and of at least one kind, the exalting and ennobling kind, of music. He recalled how he was the sun-god, and as such, associated with light and therefore with prophetic insight. Through a play upon words which, perhaps illuminatingly, links brightness with the outward appearance of things, he linked him also with fictive and imaginative creation. Again, he thought of Apollo as the god of 'ordered control, freedom from unbridled excitement, and wise serenity'.[4] Finally, because Apollo stands at the opposite pole to the god Dionysos, who represents 'the regression of individuality into...self-oblivion', Nietzsche sees Apollo as supreme representative of *what individuates*: creativity, lucidity, insight, imagination, serene wisdom, and individuality – the individually realized consciousness. Perhaps the idea, the ideal, of Apollo as a divine power under a human image, may help us to see a certain cogency in associating these ideas.

We all know that during the last hundred years or so there have been great transformations in Western art and Western literature; yet it is possible to find delight and exhilaration in twentieth-century avant-garde art and literature, and at the same time to wish to understand what has happened, and to ask if there was a price that had to be paid for the achievement of what happened. One aspect of those great transformations can be seen by recalling Piero's nativity angel, 'lost in thought' within his celestial music, and setting beside it two twentieth-century works on much the same theme. First, between about 1905 and 1930 the sculptor Jacques Lipchitz returned again and again to the subject of a human figure playing a stringed instrument. A piece like – to take one example – his 1918 *Seated Man with a Guitar* is, in his own words, using 'curved planes to create effects of interior or negative space'.[5] The human figure, and its instrument, are assembled out of rectangular, triangular or trapezoid masses, along with conic sections and what approximate to segments of a hollow sphere. Piero della Francesca would have understood all this perfectly well. Like so many of his contemporaries, he was an enthusiast for pure geometry and abstract spatial perfection. Moreover, Lipchitz's intellectual interest here in spatiality is far from altogether abstract. He goes straight on, in his discussion of this characteristic piece, to lay stress on its frontality; and the frontality of a figure has much to do with the impression of individuality which it conveys, and with its relation to others. Discussing other similar works of exactly this period, Lipchitz stresses how pure geometry and 'extreme simplification' in these works were not matters simply of (in today's language) 'solving formal problems'. He writes of another of his pieces:

the *Seated Bather* [of 1916] as a figure takes on a greater human presence. While it is still in every way an organization of plastic masses and volumes...the sense of humanity gives it a *specific personality*, a brooding quality...in this work I think I clearly achieved the kind of *poetry* which I felt to be essential in the total impact.[6]

That is true. *Seated Bather* intensely communicates the power, physical integration, inner potentiality of its subject, precisely the meditative 'ineloquence' that Berenson saw in earlier art. Apollonian reserve and power seem here to leave a place for more than themselves: they leave a place for the haunting note of a stylized but deeply individualized humanity. In all this, Lipchitz was more of an Apollonian artist than not. In 1915 or thereabouts he told Jules Romains that he 'wanted to make an art as pure as crystal'.[7] His sculpture of this period repeatedly intimates, through its very stylization, the potentiality of men, as physical objects, for dignity, upward movement, shapeliness, hard and clear-cut power. Perhaps there is a partial analogy between such work and the sculpture of Henry Moore. Why is one of Moore's most celebrated works called *King and Queen*? One may note in answer that many of his more figurative pieces could have been given the same title. Moore continually sees the regality of humanity.

Thirty years after Lipchitz's piece, the Mexican artist Rufino Tamayo painted his splendid *Man Singing* (Paris, Museum of Modern Art). Tamayo's singing figure is also playing a guitar, and is a large, post-Cubist figure, entirely filling the picture, and standing out violently, in sweeping, three-dimensional, almost black masses and curves, from the bleak and pallid cuboid space of an otherwise empty room, indicated only by the barest geometry. This picture could easily be seen as a solution to formal problems; but it also has something to say about a 'man singing'. The right hand of the singing man is simplified into a symbolic finger and thumb, a formal shape vibrant with string-plucking energy, and more like a giant metronome than a hand. The minute head on the vast tower-like neck is thrown back into a total distortion. One eye, frantic with frenzied choral participation, can just be glimpsed above the mouth, which is all glittering teeth and resonating cavity. That is the whole of what is left of the face. If ever there was a Dionysiac picture, this is one. It almost shrieks at the beholder, so totally, so intensely and all-exclusively does it embody the momentary, Dionysiac self-realization of the singer, the incarnate near-frenzy of the singing.

Momentary self-realization, realization of the momentary.

Undoubtedly, the simplifications of much twentieth-century art achieve massive intensifications of narrowed and concentrated effect; and the excitement and exhilaration of painting throughout this period lie there. Nothing would be further from the truth than to think that the termination of Rembrandtesque portraiture eventuated, in any simple way, in the evanescence of the sitter's or the single figure's personality, the collapse of his individuation. If we look at the figures in paintings of about 1920 by German Expressionists like Max Beckmann or Emil Nolde, what we sometimes find is an extraordinarily intense radiation of the individual. But it is an individuality that seems to be narrowed and concentrated. From the point of view of personality and consciousness, there is a radical simplification. Elsewhere in the painting of that period, the intensely individualized radiation seems to be transferred from what is within the work to the individuality of the artist himself. This is self-evidently the case with a great deal of non-representational art from Kandinsky on. Sometimes it is quite as true of geometric non-representational art as of what is more obviously dramatic or weighted with emotion. The Russian artist Malevich's *Black Circle* of about 1913 (Russian Museum, Leningrad) is simply a large plain black circle asymmetrically placed in the corner of a white square. His *White on White* (Museum of Modern Art, New York, 1912) depicts a white square placed slantwise across a slightly larger off-white square. Innumerable allegedly avant-garde Minimalist paintings of the 1960s advanced little or nothing upon those works. What Malevich achieved in them was to make a limited, restricted statement memorable because of its intensely, violently concentrated personal reverberation.

It is of interest to try to integrate the sense which much twentieth-century painting gives of the personality and individuality of the artist, with how also it sometimes portrays the human individual within the boundaries of the picture. Both of these dimensions often yield an intensified, concentrated image of something deliberately restricted and limited: a kind of retreat into a closed, primal power and energy. The French painter Jean Dubuffet (now long resident in the United States) is an interesting case.

Some might be able, or at least wish, to see only comedy in Dubuffet's preference for the paintings of children and the inmates of mental institutions: what he calls *art brut*, art in the raw; as also in his concocting what he has called a 'muddy paste' from sand, gravel, tar and the like, in which in part to execute his works. I am not interested in those possibilities of comedy, but should like to identify the final outcome of Dubuffet's work:

I was interested...in the brutal juxtaposition, in these female bodies, of the generalized and the particular, the subject and the object, the metaphysical and the trivial-grotesque...textures calling to mind human flesh...with other textures that...suggest rather earth and such things as bark, rocks, botanical and geographical elements...people have seen that I intend to sweep away everything that we have been taught to consider – without question – as grace or beauty; but have overlooked my work to substitute another and vaster beauty, touching all objects and beings, not excluding the most despised – and because of that, all the more *exhilarating*.[8]

Hence for example Dubuffet's 1945 *Woman Chanting* (Carlo van den Bosch Collection, Antwerp). This is at the opposite pole from Piero's music: a muddy, stylized figure, confusing skin and inwards, human body and merest object, a rock bottom of humanity. No wonder that a year or so later Dubuffet said that he 'made [his human figures] look like menhirs'.[9] Homer said that Man was a bubble. Dubuffet in effect says – but reverentially, but with solemnity, with 'ardent celebration' – Man is a stone, a piece of driftwood, a pattern in lichen. Today, we find such conceptions congenially disturbing, illuminating, and 'exhilarating'. Such works represent humanity as only just more than a random collocation of patches, blotches, swirls of *impasto* texture. Yet they reverberate with an intensity of life somehow both monumental and agonized.

This intensity speaks to us not only in respect of the

subject, but also of the artist. Dubuffet makes this point clear in his own words, writing of:

apparent mistakes...accidental blotches...forms clearly wrong, colours that don't work...I accept this because it in fact keeps one aware of the painter's hand in the picture, and prevents the object from dominating.[10]

Like many contemporary artists, Dubuffet has engaged in a considered 'Great Refusal' of the *mastery* achieved by the artists of the past.

I spoke of some of Dubuffet's representations of the human figure as 'only just more than random collocations'. The idea of the random, or more precisely the partially random, seems to demand a place in this enquiry on several different occasions. Dubuffet's later work, the *Hourloupe* series, is executed in a strange quasi-language of dotted or stippled shapes, small but extremely varied, covering the space of the picture with a unique and engrossing mosaic. Dubuffet says that this quasi-language is based on the technique of some of the most characteristic of contemporary advanced-industrial-society activities: mapping, blue-prints, circuit diagrams. But they are so based only with a difference, and a meaningful one. It is true that they make use of the techniques of mapping and the like: but they do so in arbitrary fashion. The 'map' is not for route-finding, the circuit emits no signal. They are a quasi-language only; and with them, finally and totally, the artist 'prevents the object from dominating'.

Perhaps this begins to supply what might be called a second basic equation in diagnosing the direction taken by much recent art. The first was that as representation of the object (or more still of a whole panorama of objects) recedes, registration of the artist as an individual presence tends to become more intense and insistent, but also more simple and primal. The second would be, that as objectivity and figuration recede, subjectivity and autonomy increasingly accommodate, or maybe increasingly become, partial randomness.

This is an intricate, obscure point: I feel myself discussing it with difficulty. There seem to be ways in which partial randomness promotes representativeness rather than the opposite; but then there is some kind of unstable equilibrium, with possibilities of what the musician would call an enharmonic change. Dostoevsky was reproached for departing from realism, and his reply was to turn the tables on his critics by claiming that departure from ostensible and surface realism could be a return to a profounder and completer realism. The Cubist movement in painting in the early years of the present century seems to group itself around such a moment of unstable equilibrium and enharmonic change. The earliest years of that movement, often referred to as the period of 'analytic Cubism', proposed to represent the·object more fully than hitherto; and to do this by amalgamating the various perspectives from which the object could be seen. 'Traditional perspective', wrote Braque, 'is too mechanical to allow one to *take full possession* of things.' For example, Picasso's 1909 portraits of *Fernande* (Collection Mrs Henry Church, New York, 1909) or of *Ambroise Vollard* (Moscow, Pushkin Gallery), supply the deficiency by depicting, at one and the same time, the full face and the profile of their sitters. 'Iridescence' of form is a term coined precisely to convey the sort of multiplicity, of indeterminacy without vagueness, which is the result. But over the course of only a very few years there was an interesting change, though from another perspective one could almost say that there was no change at all. The objective language that painters had developed in those early analytic Cubism days so as to 'take full possession of the object' was transformed into a subjective, non-referential language. Analytic Cubism mutated into synthetic Cubism: into the making of pictures which constituted independent, self-subsistent realities. Knowledge of, and representation of, a world of external objects no longer had anything to do with the matter. The painting invited the spectator into its own closed system. It did not any longer invite him to a larger awareness of a world of objects.

Such a change in painting had parallels in the field of literature. Apollinaire, closely linked with the Cubist painters

and himself the first writer of 'concrete poetry' – fifty years
before those who think of themselves as 'concrete
poets' – wrote:

> Certain hommes *sont des collines*
> *Qui s'élèvent d'entre les hommes*
> *Et voient au loin* tout l'avenir.

('Les Collines': *Calligrammes*)

Here, Apollinaire is taking up a thoroughly Apollonian
position about the artist: one that accords with Braque's idea
of 'taking full possession' of the external world. He sees the
artist as (in Wordsworth's phrase) a man of 'more comprehensive soul' than others, and able therefore to rise out from
among others and to see further over reality than they. He
is a Rembrandt sitter looking out from his lonely 'colline'
across the Ruisdael landscape of the world. In fact, in some
of his poems, Apollinaire may be said to approach the
super-representationalism expressed, as I noted a moment
ago, in analytic Cubism. Some of his concrete poems in
Calligrammes ('Il Pleut' and 'La Colombe Poignardée et le Jet
d'Eau' are good examples) make a picture in words as well
as a literary statement in the usual way. They assemble their
phrases in a genuine pictorial space, so that their conventional
syntactical relations, which we could compare with spatial
relations as we see them in a representational picture of the
pre-Cubist kind, are partly submerged in a spatially multiple
perspective – the object is caught all ways. Also, many of
Apollinaire's poems (such as 'A Une Jolie Rousse' of 1915)
display a fierce and powerful direct attack on the horrors of
the 1914–18 reality; they are committed poems. Yet at the
same time, Apollinaire's friend and collaborator Max Jacob
was giving the clearest possible expression to the synthetic
Cubism position, declaring that art has no connection with
conventional reality and no responsibility for it at all.[11]

Moreover, one must add a whole further dimension to
one's picture of the world of art of those uniquely formative
years. This is how artists were preoccupied with the contemporary world, with what they saw as the radically new
nature of the general reality they lived in. It is when we

recognize this that we begin to see how, in studying their ideas about art, we may well be finding out something about our own time and our own world. Perhaps the great thing is how their own preoccupation with modernity became a preoccupation with the way that modernity was incarnated in the machine. In the *Rayonniste Manifesto* of 1913, the Russian painter Larionov wrote: 'We declare: the genius of our day to be: trousers, jackets...buses...railways, magnificent ships...'[12] and at the same time said: 'We deny that individuality has any value in a work of art.' Rayonnism however was itself a reflection of Marinetti's first *Futurist Manifesto* of four years before: 'A racing car is more beautiful than the Victory of Samothrace'[13] – he of course meant the sculpture in the Louvre. The admiration of the Cubist painters, and also Apollinaire, for dynamism in art makes a link between Cubism and other art movements like Futurism and Rayonnism. And all these points have a rather surprising conclusion, though one that I have already approached. The Cubists' admiration for geometry, and also for dynamism in art, the Futurists' and Rayonnists' preoccupation with movement and the machine, both lead back to the concept of partial randomness as a key concept in respect of twentieth-century art.

We must contrast randomness, or partial randomness, both with human decision and choice comprehensively exercised, and with the often total determinism of a machine as it operates. But the enthusiasm of the early twentieth century for the machine was not for its determinism: rather, for its dynamism, speed and movement. As soon as the cult of dynamism calls on the artist to represent movement, the range of arbitrary choice becomes wider for him. Much the same thing happens if a Cubist aesthetic calls upon him to amalgamate a multiplicity of viewpoints.

Consider one or two examples, like Luigi Russolo's lost nightpiece, entitled *A Train at High Speed*, of about 1910. Russolo in this painting broke up anything like photographic representation. He conveyed not only the movement of the train as that would be seen from outside by someone watching it speed by, but also the impression of the night-time lights of the landscape, as seen from inside the train. Result, there is an effect like that of a cinematograph running slow but accelerating, just as its flicking and flickering merge into smooth motion-picture realism. Needless to say, the cinematograph was coming into its own in the very years when Russolo was painting this picture. Russolo conveyed these effects by dissolving the lights of both his train, and his landscape, into a kind of rushing, swirling confusion. As he did so, the object represented ceased fully to determine his picture; and that freedom to choose resulted in an arbitrariness, partially ordered, but also partially random.

Likewise with Severini's masterpiece of 1910 – also a lost work – entitled *Danse du Pan-Pan à Monico*. This was an extraordinary scene of dynamic movement, composed of, as it were, mere fragments, in hundreds, of diners in a café where everything is half-submerged in a colourful jungle and jumble of innumerable dancing arms, legs, and faces, skipping and leaping, disjoined from their bodies, lost in the jubilant mêlée. Again, the picture is far indeed from being wholly random in its organization. Clearly the artist was constrained by certain formal considerations: for example, none of the fragments in this vast aggregation of fragments is much larger than any other. He also felt the constraint of certain representational considerations: none of the heads is painted upside-down. Yet for all that, the impression given by the picture is that dancing humanity is a largely random aggregation, even perhaps that it is exhilarating because of its randomness.

One further example will show that this conception of partial randomness sometimes holds good of more or less representational works. Kasimir Malevich's painting *Scissors Grinder* (1912, in the Yale Gallery) disintegrates the physical materiality of the grinder's hands and feet, and of the treadle of his machine, of his moving leg and of the revolving wheel. All this is transformed into movement and splutter – the tensed dynamism, the flash and spark and sharp harsh noise of the mechanical process, all rendered in the language of paint. But a remarkable fact emerges as one continues to study this picture. True enough, there is an element of randomness in every part of the picture without exception. Even when he represents the knife-grinder's fingers, Malevich feels free to put them in threes, or in fours, or in fives, or in sevens, to suggest how they vibrate and shudder in the grinding process. But as the eye moves outward from the key elements at the centre – which have a prominent representational aspect and which after all have supplied the picture with its title – towards the periphery of the picture, it is impossible not to think that the element of arbitrariness or randomness in the selection increases. At the edges, in the corners, we find ourselves looking at an almost wholly abstract painting (which of course is not to say, a wholly random one). Somewhere, admittedly, there are hints of a stairway, a balustrade. Certainly, the symbolic white square recurrent in Malevich's paintings is half-visible.[14] In the main, though, formal considerations alone underlie choice and selectiveness, and therefore make possible an art which combines order with a considerable measure of the random. This point holds good generally of the work of Braque or Juan Gris, even their analytic Cubism works. One could put it in brief by saying that the edges of such works become synthetic Cubism, become in effect abstract, before the middles.

Aleatory art, therefore, the art of free or at least of partially free choice, seems to have arrived with those movements in the early part of this century which glorified the machine and its dynamism; and the 'oscillation' technique of abstract Impressionism recalls the 'iridescence' of Cubism. What time since the beginning of the century has significantly added takes us back to Dubuffet, and stresses how partial randomness does not mean depersonalization in any simple or total way; it too can perfectly well express the artist's personality at least on certain terms. Moreover, time has added a variety of more or less sophisticated techniques for achieving partial randomness, necessary because an artist can intend randomness a good deal more easily than he can achieve it unaided. So, in 1976, we find Ellen B. Johnson, in *Modern Art and the Object*, writing about 'drip painting', and saying 'this way of painting is more than an indifference to traditional technique: it is a positive style created deliberately to affirm *freshness, immediacy*, and the *excitement* of forces in tension'.[15]

The point is that now, when the artist thinks of how to express himself, how to 'affirm', what he thinks of is affirming freshness, immediacy, and excitement. How far that is from what Rembrandt or Piero della Francesca thought a man had it in him to affirm! When Jackson Pollock writes 'it seems to be possible to control the flow of paint, *to a great extent*, and I don't use...the accident...I deny the accident', or 'I do have a *general notion* of what I'm about', he is denying that his works are random products, but he is clearly confirming the suggestion that, as with a good deal of modern art, though doubtless in varying ways, the order created is an order of partial randomness.[16]

Sometimes we overlook how widely the concept of partial randomness is applicable in all forms of art – the critic's first reaction is to identify it with chaos, whereas it is really a somewhat sophisticated kind of order. In particular, the concept of partial randomness seems to apply quite widely to literature. That is, the ways in which certain of the items in the literary work might be transposed, and yet no one be able to say that the work had been impaired in some specific and clearly identifiable way; or even that its total meaning had identifiably been changed. One feature of passages in heroic couplets, for example, is that the individual couplets may sometimes – to a limited extent only – be transposed and the whole not be significantly changed. Tennyson's 132 'short swallow-flights of song' in *In Memoriam* present a similar case. Of course there is an overall design, of course many transpositions would alter or impair that design. But it is impossible to claim out of hand that all without exception would do so. Hence one is obliged to recognize that there is an element of partial randomness in the organization of that poem.

From certain literary works, Horace's *Odes* for example, or Hölderlin's written in imitation of them, such transpositions are excluded to a maximum degree. That that is so is part of their poetic effect, and part doubtless of their author's intention. But for the present discussion, the crucial point is that two of the major innovations of recent poetry almost necessarily increase the element of partial randomness in the poem. These are, free verse, and composition simply by juxtaposing syntactically unconnected items: what Ezra Pound called the 'mode of superposition'. Eliot could not possibly have transposed any of the five whole sections of *The Waste Land*. It is not self-evident, however, that if he had transposed the 'Hyacinth Girl' and 'Madame Sosostris' passages in Part I, the poem would necessarily have been impaired, or even that its meaning would have been significantly modified. If in Part II he had written:

> My nerves are bad tonight. Yes, bad. Stay with me.
> Speak to me. Why do you never speak?
>
> What is that noise?
>   The wind under the door.
>
> What is that noise now? What is the wind doing?
>   Nothing again nothing.
>
> What are you thinking of? What thinking? What?
> I never know what you are thinking. Think.
>
>   Do
> You know nothing? Do you see nothing? Do you
> remember nothing?
>
> I think we are in rats' alley
> Where the dead men lost their bones.

– if Eliot had written that, by no means every reader of Eliot would be able to show what had been lost, or even changed.

Likewise in Pound's *Cantos*, or Williams's *Paterson*, or Olson's *Maximus* poems. Where laconic or cryptic juxtapositions of discrete or even of barely related items is the mode of writing, transposition enters as a possibility, and the order of the work is a partially random order. To say so is not to fault such works, any more than it is, to detect a similar mode of order in certain Cubist or other twentieth-century paintings; nevertheless, it is certainly to recognize another mode of deviation from that all-comprehending order of mind which has been called 'Apollonian'.

Viewed in general terms, there are three qualities which may be distinguished in the art, and the literature, of the present century, and which seem to point in a certain direction. These are, a recession of concern with the object, and especially with awareness of external reality as a whole integrated order of externality (as in the great Dutch landscapes); an emphasis on intensity, immediacy and spontaneity; and an increased partial randomness. Is it possible that there are significant parallels to this, again in somewhat general terms, over the whole texture of our ordinary life? With regard to contemporary leanings towards spontaneity, 'immediacy' and 'excitement', there is no need to labour the point. It may seem strange to speak of a recession of concern with external reality and the external order. Some may suppose that modern man has mastered his environment, and done so for the first time in history. But consider the situation of someone in an apartment of thoroughly contemporary design and furnishing, asked to give the exactly correct name of every material substance around him in the room, and to summarize how it was made into the article that he sees before him. The fact is, most of us today live in a physical environment that we barely begin to comprehend at all, or even in the full sense to identify.

As for partial randomness, one thinks of the immense range of choice that contemporary life offers, and also of the limits to that choice. We are entirely free to park our car in any of the maybe hundreds of vacant places in a parking-lot, and the limitations upon that choice are inconspicuous – we cannot for instance park in a lead-free atmosphere. We can take a pleasure-drive along any of scores of well-maintained roads, all that we probably cannot do is find a lonely one. In the supermarket we can reach out our hand at random among innumerable commodities (often all much the same), and it does not occur to us that there are certain things we are unable to buy, like silence for the rest of the day, or the chance to do something we shall think truly worthwhile.

Choice is wonderfully free, and so are we free to be our spontaneous selves. But we are less free to be our reflecting selves. If we wish to try to choose that all-composing, all-comprehending, Apollonian totality of life which I have had in mind, things are not the same.

II   COMIC ART, CODED CARTOON

I F   W E   T U R N from the serious art to the comic art
of the past century or thereabouts, it is natural to begin by
thinking about the work of George du Maurier, certainly the
foremost of English cartoonists of the later nineteenth
century. Du Maurier joined the staff of *Punch*, at the age of
thirty, in 1864. By this time *Punch* had been running for
over twenty years, and had already become a national
institution in Britain. Du Maurier as a young man had been
an art student, and doubtless he would have become a
professional Victorian painter had he not, at age 23, lost the
sight of his left eye. The hundreds of comic illustrations that
he drew for *Punch* in the course of his career show his
mastery of the whole panorama of Victorian life. His power
as a humorist strikes the reader in the first place through
his power to represent, by the most delicate touches of
ironical caricature, his subjects' faultlessly snow-white linen
and beautifully cut clothes (many of his jokes introduce
tailors and dressmakers), the men's abundant Victorian
sideburns, moustaches and beards, the women's exquisitely
elaborate hair-dressing.

Also, he knew exactly how people held their hats, canes,
cigarettes, golf-clubs, parasols, fans or muffs, just how a
footman held his single glove, how a haughty little Miss
drooped her eyelids ('Uncle George says every woman ought
to have a profession...I mean to be a professional beauty');
and he seems to know how to define, for good and all, by
this panoramic encyclopaedia of detail, the old-fashioned
well-bred man ('our friend the gallant Colonel', who appears
repeatedly in his cartoons), the pompous upper-class re-
actionary (Sir Pompey Bedell), the self-important nouveau-
riche (Sir Gorgias Midas), and the young aesthetes and
exquisites of *art nouveau*.[17] One of his exquisites says that he

25

is looking for a wife, and has his eye on the younger Miss Godwin; not the elder, because the younger would go better with the *Buhl*, and the *marqueterie* furniture, that this young hero has been collecting in his bachelor apartment.

Du Maurier knows all about *Buhl* and *marqueterie* himself; as also about the couches, lavish curtains, potted palms, dados, chandeliers, cheval-glasses, trays, grand pianos, all the other Victoriana. His social satire is a delicate web of how his people stand, sit, loll or lean forward in gentlemanly attentiveness, or absurd aesthetic yearning, as they navigate their way through the bric-à-brac plethora of their houses. A single drawing may have fifteen or twenty faces, each of them sharply individualized, each of them drawing in its own way upon its author's voluminious and microscopic knowledge. In one drawing of an evening party listening to amateur music, the faces express supercilious reserve, deep Germanic concentration, or jealousy at skill displayed; while another is yawning, another falling asleep, another again conscious only of his handsome profile. The reader must read the drawing in these terms. He must fill his mind with this inexhaustible detail of both the outer and the inner life of the Victorian panorama. Often enough, du Maurier deploys such a knowledge, or calls for it, extending well beyond the drawing itself. 'Who are those two men in hats and white coats?', asks one enchanting Victorian beauty of another, watching cricket at Lords and looking, of course, at the two umpires. 'They', comes the reply from her friend, 'are the headmasters of Eton and Harrow.'

It is the same with what his characters say. Of course, they are given to dialogue which by today's standards seems prolix; but very largely, du Maurier makes his humour out of the fine local touches of Victorian life. The father of 'Young Hopeful' accuses his son of ignorance. 'But why did you send me to a Public School?', comes the reply, 'I always look upon a fellow who's learnt anything at a Public School as *a self-educated man*!' 'We've come to see the acting, we do not wish to understand the play', says a Victorian lady to a hawker who tries to sell her a *libretto*: the respectable Victorian attends the theatre with caution. The new American

governess explains that she will not be able to teach the
young ladies foreign languages with a good accent; but
there is no call for that; what she is there for is to give their
English an American accent, so that they may have a chance
to *marry English dukes*. 'You're not the boy I left my horse
with', says the elderly gentleman to what was once known
as a youthful 'street-arab': 'No sir, I *speculated*, and bought
him from the other boy for a *half*-penny', is the reply. The
infant face of Victorian capitalism.

A significant part of du Maurier's knowledge, and so of
his humour, concerns the English language itself in his time.
'Bless you my lady! May we meet in Heaven!', says the
grateful mother of a rustic family to the elderly alms-giver
in her carriage. But for the latter, to 'meet' has primarily
social connotations. 'Good gracious! Drive on, Jarvis', says
her Ladyship to the coachman. Du Maurier has made
humour from playing one of the clichés of Victorian English
off against its double: meet at a dinner party, meet in
Heaven. Elsewhere 'Our gallant Colonel' tells his partner at
a dinner party that the engaged couple across the room have
both had distinguished academic careers at Cambridge. How
different their conversation must be, she replies, from the
insipid twaddle of ordinary lovers. But du Maurier's humour,
in this case, is again a matter of the detail of consciousness
that he locates in those he depicts. What the Cambridge
mathematician really had to say to his enchanting Girton
blue-stocking was: 'And what would *Dovey* do if *Lovey* were
to die?' When the natty gent. goes into a merchant's shop
to buy printing-*type*, he refers to it as 'tape', and the
assistant, when at last he understands, calls it 'toipe'. Such
were – still are – the vagaries of pronunciation in English
English, the fine detail of the English social landscape.

Over and over, du Maurier's captions depend for their
humour upon picking up the faint overtones of cliché in the
speech of his time. 'May I ask you', says a departing guest
to the nervous hostess of the evening, 'to get one of your
people to find me a carriage?'; 'With *pleasure*, madam!', the
poor woman unthinkingly replies. 'Mama, shall you let me
go to the Wilkinson's ball...this winter?', asks the daughter.

'No, darling.' 'You've been to a great many balls, haven't you Mama?' 'Yes darling – and I've *seen the folly* of them all.' 'Mightn't I just see the folly of *one?*' This is the humour of the Victorian novelist (du Maurier of course was that too): omnivorous, exact, sensitive to all the finer and individuated shades of meaning, or non-meaning, in the speech of his time.

Especially, perhaps, du Maurier revelled in the overtones and follies of the Aesthetic Movement. There is for example the craze for old china. The daughter – one of six daughters, we see all these ravishing children in the background – tells her weeping, heart-broken mother, who has dropped an artistic teapot, not to take on so. 'You still have *me*', she childishly but aptly says. But the mother wails in reply, 'you're not *unique*...you're one of a *set!*' Listening to an evening party violin sonata, the 'enthusiastic young lady' says to her earth-of-the-earth-earthy partner, 'Does it not strike you, listening to sweet music, that the rudiment of potential infinite pain is subtly woven into the tissue of our keenest joy?' These are the inner raptures of Shelley's *Skylark*, watered down through endless Victorian socialite gatherings. In one of du Maurier's 'Distinguished Amateur' series ('The Art-Critic', *Punch*, 1890) we have the tones of Ruskin's art criticism, (or Pater on Leonardo). The youthful Prigsby is lecturing his bevy of admiring languid beauties: 'Distinctly divine', he says; 'Nor can I, in the whole range of Ancient, Medieval or Modern Art, recall anything quite so fair and precious...unless it be...that supremest master-piece of Greek Sculptchah...whereof indeed, in a certain gracious modelling of the lovely Neck, and in the subtly delectable curves of the Cheek and Chin, it faintly, yet most exquisitely reminds me!' All this about the head of an Antique Greek piece that is in fact headless. Repeatedly, du Maurier's humour comes from his ironical portrayal of what, elsewhere, appeared as the serious intimacies of consciousness.

'Exquisite', 'quite' and 'consummate' are prominent in the vocabulary of du Maurier's aesthetes. What the admiring young ladies say when Fitz-Lavender Belairs reads them his dreadful Swinburnian verse is: 'How really quite too far more than most awfully delicious!' 'Are you *intense?*', are the first words of an aesthetic lovely to the singularly prosaic-looking young man who has been asked by the hostess to take her in to dinner. Du Maurier's reader is a type distinctively conceived. The humour that he is invited to enjoy calls for an ability and willingness not simply to know the difference between a nincompoop, a prig, a swell, and a true gentleman in terms of the conduct, attitudes and language of the time, but also to be conscious of the whole spectrum of personality and individuality, male or female, as those things define themselves through fine shades of contemporaneity: the dress, bearing and speech of the time.

Du Maurier was perhaps the last great English cartoonist of quite this kind. In 1884, when du Maurier was at the height of his powers, appeared the first English magazine to publish a strip cartoon – a 'comic strip'; *Ally Sloper's Half-Holiday*. In this weekly, like *Comic Cuts* and *Chips*, which both started publication six years later, the basic recipes for the items are much the same as those on which du Maurier relied. Insofar as the more limited skills of the artists (and, one suspects, of the printers) allowed, the characters presented in the illustrations, including the comic strips, are intended here too as vividly and cleverly individualized. The humour often arises out of current idiom, just as du Maurier's did. The age of puns is not over, though the puns are minimal indeed – one of the earliest strips, about an athletics match, was entitled 'A Running Tale'. 'I understand the art of hanging pictures', says the self-important husband to his dutifully attendant wife, 'right down to the ground.' Needless to say (for our own sophisticated palates), at this moment he falls off the step-ladder. There is not much dividend for us in the joke, but the fact remains that it is the detail of contemporary life, personality, manners and 'language-usage' that are supplying the humour, such as it is. Ally Sloper himself, as well as Weary Willy and Tired Tim (in *Chips*) are Dickensian characters. Timpkins in *Comic Cuts*, the office clerk who moves out into the country, is a little like Dickens's character Wemmick in *Great Expectations*.

The distinction from du Maurier is that his humour is prepared for those who are interested in the lives of the lower and lower middle, not the upper classes; and also that the skill of those producing the magazine is less.

In the end, this last point had significant results: for even in the early comics, character and consciousness come often to be distinguished through *stylization*. Stylization has of course occurred in art from the earliest times; and to a greater or lesser extent it occurs, and it must as a physical necessity occur, in almost all art – or at least visual art. It is a mistake, though, to think that all stylization works in the same way or has the same kind of significance. If one looks closely at a Rembrandt portrait, or a landscape by one of Rembrandt's Dutch contemporaries (still more, if one looks with a magnifying lens) it becomes very clear that the painter has stylized many of the details – hair, for example, or wrinkles, or in the landscapes, the semi-transparency of water). These stylizations, however, are not meant to be noticed. They are necessary because of the small scale of the painting or the nature of paint itself; or perhaps to economize time, or for some other similar reason. The primary intention is clearly that they should escape the spectator's attention. Instead of noticing these stylizing features, he is meant to respond as if what were before him were a full record, not a simplified record of reality. The invitation is to become immersed in its fullness, not to detect and enjoy the neatness or ingenuity of its departures from that. In such works, stylization is not meant to interfere with a final impression of indefinitely great depth and richness, of plenitude calling out the complete range of the spectator's mind and all his powers of reflection and meditation.

The stylization of the comic strip is different (and the stylization of much contemporary art is to a certain degree like it). In the comic strip, the intention is that we should be saved trouble, and perhaps also should recognize the artist's effectiveness and skill in saving us trouble. We are to be given a clear but simplified message, in circumstances when simplification is all that we need for as much of the situation or story as gives us the humour; and the humour is itself of a clearly, conveniently delimited kind. We need not pore over the drawing, and are not invited to pore over it for the most part; because, for our convenience, it has been stylized so as to be receivable without difficulty or even without effort.

In the comic strips, stylization came to be widely used to give a simple, no-trouble-to-follow presentation of human consciousness, personality and emotion. Raised eyebrow, circular open mouth, meant surprise; down-turned line for the mouth, disapproval, vexation, concern; outsize feet or rigidly straddled legs meant confidence or a firm stance. Today these shorthand devices are second nature to all. The treatment of the hands was particularly interesting. Du Maurier usually seeks to make his characters' hands subtly, individually expressive of character or passing mood. But hands are difficult to draw, and even he sometimes falls into sketchiness over hands, or seems to be saving himself trouble by the use of pockets, in which those awkward items may be conveniently got out of the way.

But the minor comic artists in Britain at the turn of the century take that further. Often, their drawing of hands is plain incompetent. Not infrequently, they get them out of sight. But the main point is how simplified, stylized hands begin to come regularly into the drawings: the admonitory or pointing outstretched index finger; the threatening clenched fist that expresses either threat or resolve; the open hand, fingers together, at arm's length, to draw attention to something; or with fingers apart, to mean falling, help-lessness, or astonishment. Again, happy smiles are sym-metrical, mischievous smiles are one-sided. To indicate close attention, or listening, or bewilderment, the mouth is omitted. Other drawing conventions of the comic strip include symbols for movement, being precariously balanced, being hit, potential energy (like big muscles), jumping, being giddy, swearing, other explosions, and all the rest. These are familiar to us today.

One by one, these are of trifling interest. Taken together, they show that comic illustration was developing a means of expression and communication very different from that relied upon by du Maurier and by most earlier comic illustrators and cartoonists. What we are encountering, in fact, is the development of an overt *code* for conventionalized expression of the story-line, the responses of the people depicted, and the humour. The connection with the previous chapter will by now be clear: we are identifying another direction along which the representation of full individuality and personally realized consciousness is being replaced by something made deliberately simpler, more radical, and perhaps more intense (in a context like this one would be more inclined to say something that 'packs more punch'). The reader no longer finds an invitation to recognize an 'inner' individuality and to do something by way of constructing the consciousness of a character, as in some Victorian novels. He does not have to move comparatively deeply in thought, to expand his own consciousness in order to become inward with that other consciousness. He learns to read messages in a simple code based on a number of diagrammatizations of experience.

Several lines of development may be traced in these comic codes. One for example concerns feminine attractiveness. On a few strip cartoons (like *Tiffany Jones*, a British cartoon drawn by two women) the codification is minimal or rather it is distinctive. As I think everyone knows, however, if a woman came into the room displaying the exact proportions and postures of the women drawn in many comic strips, they would seem almost deformed. In the drawings, we simply read off a code that says: 'attractive girl'. We are not looking for close representations of real-life attractiveness at all. *Wonder Woman*, with her immensely long legs, was an especially interesting case from this point of view, because the artist who drew her had the problem of amalgamating the attractive-girl code with another code that has long been important in the comics: that of heroic super-strong masculinity. All are by now familiar with the items constituent of this latter code: wide straight mouth, square jaw-line, hypertrophy of leg-length, impossible muscular over-development and indeed mis-development. This code runs from *Li'l Abner* through *Tarzan* (begun 1929), *Garth*,

Steve Canyon, Dan Dare, Superman (1938), *The Torch, Batman, Green Arrow* and *Captain America*. In another context than the present one, it would be of interest to classify the signals which differentiate the super-hero from the super-villain. *Popeye*'s enlarged fore-arms are a guy, I think, upon one part of the super-man code: they offer a code-sign for another code-sign. Critics who like to speak of a meta-code have here a chance to do so.

Perhaps a special interest attaches to Norman Pett's comic strip, *Jane*, which began in the British *Daily Mirror* in 1932. *Jane* was enormously popular during the Second World War, and was the darling of the armed forces. But the point I have particularly in mind is that in several of the books of *Jane* cartoons which Pett published after the war, there are a number of full-length photographs of the actual model used by the artist. The photographs show Pett's model as exceptionally well-developed; but a little scholarly analysis of this naked lady, as she appears in the photographs, by comparison with how she is drawn in the cartoons, reveals some of the detail of how Pett encoded her in his work. Obviously one cannot measure circumference in either photographs or drawings; but when this model is shown fully facing the camera, or turned fully away from it, the ratio of her width across the waist to the distance from her hip joint to her knee is 1:1.75. That is indeed a well-proportioned arrangement. In the drawings, however, the ratio is never less than 1:2.6, and it goes up to 1:2.9. Still more striking is what Pett did in regard to the hands and the eyes. His model had rather small eyes – he regularly drew them as large and very firmly marked – and she had shapely, rather large hands, with perhaps slightly oversize palms and a well-developed little finger. In the drawings, Jane's hands have impossibly small palms, and willowy fingers with one joint only. These fingers are tapered almost throughout their whole length, I think to suggest long tapering nails, a point too small to show realistically in the drawings. The little finger is always drawn very small, and not infrequently shown in positions which really could only mean that it was dislocated backwards at the knuckle-joint.

The tapering fingers and small palms make Jane's hands, as drawn, look like starfish, and really rather repulsive, if attended to closely. But 'attended to closely' is a misleading phrase. It means, 'seen in a realistic convention' instead of 'seen in the convention of the strip code'.

A third development of the comic strip constituted a more significant move away from the ample treatment of consciousness as in du Maurier. This development has relied on a *dramatis personae* of children, animals and adults – like comic-doll figures: for example *Bringing Up Father*, started by George McManus in 1913, and the rather similar *Pop*, drawn by J. Millar Watt and first appearing in the *Daily Sketch* in 1921. With those would go a comic strip like *Blondie and Dagwood*, begun by Chic Young in 1930 and still running (of course drawn by other artists), though to my eye it now looks somewhat old-fashioned. With these may be considered animal comic strips like George Herriman's *Krazy Kat* with Ignatz Mouse and the half-human Offissa Pupp; *Pogo* with his duckling, bear and alligator companions; and from 1950 on, Charlie, Lucy and the other children who, with the dog Snoopy, make up the *Peanuts* cortège.

At first it may seem as if *Bringing Up Father*, *Pop*, and the animal strips ought hardly to be considered together; but they all have a fundamental feature in common. They all, and recurrently, make the same sort of contrast with the type of illustrated comedy that draws on (as I put it earlier) 'consciousness of the whole spectrum of personality and individuality'. Pop's most characteristic humour, for example, is a kind of vestigial humour. The settings and furnishings in which he lives are vestigial, or often simply non-existent. In the main, he himself is inarticulate. His inner life is made up simply of telling scraps. He looks at a splendid rainbow, grunts, 'Isn't that lovely?', and at once walks away. 'Are you asleep?', his talkative wife asks him in the small hours. 'Yes', he firmly but imprudently replies, taking the wish for the deed. On the whole, there is a certain formulaic idea that is fundamental to most of the humour in this strip, and it is exactly to the point. It is, that the 'fine consciousness' is expendable. In everyday life, a kind of straightforward stupidity can more than survive. 'When you get run down, go for a walk', pontificates the doctor. 'It's when I go for a walk I get run down', Pop replies. So little individuality is required to 'get by'. This type of humour was not unknown to the Victorian illustrators. There used to be dialogue between an uneducated small boy and an older person that ended with the parenthetical phrase 'collapse of elderly gent'. It is much to the point in this discussion that a 'smart' but illiterate child is the nearest analogue in earlier comic illustration to the elderly figure of Pop.

A great deal of the dialogue in the *Peanuts* strip is like this, and shows how the 'animal' strip cartoon can be like those with 'minimal' humans. '"Where did you get those statistics?" says Patty to Charlie. "I just made them up."' Elsewhere, Charlie complains to Lucy: 'You don't like me – well, you don't think I'm perfect.' Over long stretches of this *roman fleuve*, the dog Snoopy is governed by quite rigid and sophisticated conventions. This dog can think fluently in language, and understand it perfectly; only he can't speak. In other words, he is what many people think their own dogs are like. 'There is the disadvantage of having a limited vocabulary', thinks Snoopy, on hearing the humans ask themselves why he barked all night. Relatively speaking, he is a passive and static dog. He can walk in a clockwork sort of way, but for any greater speed is usually drawn as if propelled by some invisible mechanism. He constantly falls off his kennel roof when asleep on it. He is regularly defeated by birds, butterflies, leaves, or the wind. Only the humans are even less resourceful, even more crude and primitive and simplified in nature, than he is; in the main, he can hold his own against them, or more, by silence. 'Other dogs go to bed without having a piggy back ride!' they complain at him, unavailingly.

In short, he is a smart but inarticulate child, who constantly causes the 'collapse' of the human ladies or gents. Some of his remarks would fit well into a *Pop* strip. 'I'm independent... well, sort of semi-independent'; 'listening to someone else always depresses me'; 'our own food is the most important thing'; 'I'm a cat-hater, a cat-loather, a cat-despiser, I'm also scared to death of them': with Pop one must substitute 'mother-in-law' for 'cat'. In other words, Snoopy represents not perhaps our worst, but our weakest self: what we are like when we are too tired to go to bed, or when we are ill and childish, or before we have pulled ourselves together on waking up; but, he represents that weakest self winning, not losing. So, strip cartoons like these bring in the polar opposite of the Apollonian consciousness. They involve a rudimentary consciousness, made up of rudimentary needs, weaknesses, desires, resentments, self-satisfactions. They show us, whether in outspoken children, half-bewildered old men, or pseudo-animals, minds unmodulated by all the fine texturing that comes from training, history, social change, self-discipline or intellectual and emotional development.

George Herriman's *Krazy Kat* series, perhaps the finest comic strip of all, was based upon much the same sort of fundamental idea. Everything is simplified and codified. Offissa Pupp grows two fingers when he does a painting, otherwise his hands are like boxing gloves. Ignatz Mouse has arms, hands and legs of wire. His tail is also wire. Krazy Kat's tail is a walking-stick. Mouths disappear. All that happens, happens against the monstrous backcloth, timeless but variable (be it noted) quite at random, of the Arizona Desert. Here, Ignatz Mouse endlessly throws his brick at Krazy Kat – always with about the same action – and Krazy Kat always takes it for love. I suppose we know that such an arrangement, when the two people in question are simple enough, can stand for truth not falsehood. Between them, they eternally get the better of Offissa Pupp the human; and I suppose we know that that could represent a truth too. It has been said that *Peanuts* is a world of children who 'intensify adult ideas'.[18] If that is right, it is at least equally right of Krazy Kat. One pauses over that formulation, because what was learnt in one's formative years was that it was Shakespeare, Racine, Tolstoy, James, Faulkner and the others who intensified adult ideas. Certainly it was such achievement as theirs that Coleridge had in mind when he coined the very word 'intensify'. But if it is true that the comic strip of recent years, by simplifying through use of the child or the animal, by reducing the responses it depicts to the absolutely minimal and rudimentary, indeed achieves an 'intensification' of ideas, then the contrast with major comic artists of a century ago is clear. What is more, the parallel, also, is surely clear, between the transition in the comic strip which I have been following out in this chapter, and the transitions in more serious art that were the concern of the previous one.

III CONSCIOUSNESS AND THE LANGUAGE OF POLITICS, 1880–1980

As a preliminary to discussing the language, over the past hundred years or so, of political oratory and debate, and how that language suggests something in regard to the theme of this book, certain possible misunderstandings should be noticed and set aside.

First, the question will not be of how much store politicians have set upon the potential range and wealth of human consciousness – its Apollonian powers – deliberately, and as part of their overt political programmes. Such matters are unlikely to figure prominently in anyone's political programme; and, moreover, most or all politicians, at least over the period in question, would pay homage to them (though it might sometimes be mere lip-service) if challenged. The question will rather be of what their own language indirectly suggests or reveals about their conceptions of individual consciousness, in themselves or in others, when their overt thoughts are elsewhere.

It should also be understood that no conclusions are implied by the present discussion about the adequacy or otherwise of the work of the politicians and speakers considered here, in respect of their political contributions viewed generally. If it should transpire that responsiveness to the range of human consciousness seems to have declined, that is not intended to imply any decline in general political competence. The intention is to leave that open. I ought also to mention that most of the political oratory and debate considered in this chapter comes from the Liberal, or later the Labour side. Conservative politicians are quoted only incidentally and infrequently. The reason for this restriction is a very simple one. If one were to quote without restraint from speakers of all parties, it would be difficult not to reveal one's own political preferences, and probably difficult not to seem at least to discriminate in favour of one particular party, in respect of the matters under consideration. Nothing is further from my wishes than that, so it seemed the least misleading or confusing course to choose one 'side', as it were, in politics, and for present purposes the choice may be seen as an arbitrary one.

Perhaps I should make one further preliminary point. Politicians – of whatever complexion – are sometimes thought to be capable of a measure of cynicism. If so, they can doubtless refer in their speeches to deep thought, comprehensive vision, inwardness, profound feeling and so forth, yet care less for those things than their words imply. Such a possibility, however, proves to be irrelevant to the matters now at issue. Whether a speaker pays genuine homage, or calculated lip-service, to certain values and ideas, in either case it is clear not only that such ideas and values will be familiar to him in some sense, but also that he thinks they will be both familiar to his hearers, and prized by them. If he thought that they would prove as indifferent as he was himself, he would not be at the trouble of speaking as he does.

So, cynicism would, of course, make a certain difference, but it would make no decisive difference. All the time, we are concerned with aspects of humanity and of its consciousness that people will take (or fail to take) for granted, as easily as they will insist explicitly upon them; and that they will bring to light unconsciously, or at the fringes of consciousness, by the exact quality of the language they use as they speak of other things: their 'turns of phrase' as they speak of matters within the field of 'practical politics' and its immediate concerns.

With those preliminary points in mind, consider some words of Gladstone's in 1884 and, alongside them, something said by Harold Wilson in 1965. Both politicians were speaking in the House of Commons, on subjects to which they attached great importance. Gladstone was commenting on the matter of General Gordon in the Sudan; he referred to begin with to one of his colleagues, who had spoken, he said, of:

what he deemed to be a just position on this subject – namely, that we ought to make up our minds as to that which we deem to be necessary...and having made up our minds, to adhere firmly to the intention so formed.

(*Hansard*, 23 October 1884: subsequent references to Parliamentary speeches will be from *Hansard* and give date only.)

Somewhat later in the same speech, Gladstone used the following words:

it is but right that, without anger or warmth, I should express what I sorrowfully believe to be the true construction of the right hon Gentleman's words.

Rightly or wrongly, the tone of Gladstone's remarks does not automatically command immediate assent today. Even so, they make a significant contrast with some remarks made in Parliament by Harold Wilson, when Prime Minister, in connection with a subject quite as momentous as Gladstone's, the unilateral declaration of independence by Rhodesia (now Zimbabwe):

Mr Smith...went on to say that...he took it that it would not be right of him if he did not tell me that the feeling seemed to be that it looked as though this thing had gone too far.

(11 November 1965: H. Wilson, *Purpose in Power*, 1966, pp. 159–60).

A few sentences later, Harold Wilson said:

I ended the telephone conversation with a heavy heart feeling that reason had fled the scene and that emotion...had taken command.

These two passages warrant reflection. Here on the one hand we have Gladstone and his contemporaries, and on the other, Harold Wilson and Ian Smith. In each case, whether at first or second hand, we have something of what was said by all. True enough, it is one comparative example only, but in a way that strikes the mind and is food for thought, the comparison seems to throw larger issues into relief. Gladstone, in both of the remarks quoted above, is setting a conspicuous value on 'firm', close thought, on the mental formulation of a clear opinion, and on the avoidance of distracting emotion. That is clear from his language – 'deem', 'just position', 'true construction' and so on. For Gladstone the task of the politician is to let his mind reflect carefully and with concentration, and then to express his considered findings as lucidly and rationally as he can. That, at least by implication, Wilson also sets store by reason (he had a 'heavy heart' because it 'fled the scene'), and that he deprecates emotion taking command, only emphasizes the contrast between them. It is quite possible that Smith's vacuous and serpentine monstrosity ('this thing had gone too far') was – by him – intended to avoid substantial communication, not achieve it. But Wilson seems to have felt no Gladstonian obligation to 'express...the true construction' of Smith's words, to 'make up our minds' about that. Those words seem to have served, as they stood, to carry his hearers along more or less without effort of mind; and one must add that Wilson's own comments, relying on such catch-phrases as 'heavy heart', 'reason had fled the scene' (a theatrical cliché?) and 'emotion...had taken command', leave us with a similar impression, once we reflect upon them. Furthermore, it is not the catch-phrases themselves as much as how they pack easily together and how little weight they are given, which is the telling point; and the contrast is with how Gladstone gave emphasis and deliberateness to his 'true construction'. That point is unaffected by how Gladstone's language strikes a modern reader as a trifle antiquated – and in fact, I do not know whether this detracts from the impression of capacious deliberateness in his words, or accentuates it. I also hope there is no need to repeat that the discussion in no way reflects adversely upon Wilson's political adequacy over the 1965 crisis: it is perfectly possible to argue that the subtlety of mind, or the awareness which is here being explored is, or has become, either an irrelevance, or an embarrassment, in practical politics.

What is beginning to transpire, in fact, is that it is, as it were, at the 'periphery' of their speeches, or their writings, rather than in the substance of what they say, that politicians reveal most about their attitudes to thought or consciousness or emotion. By 'periphery', I chiefly mean those incidental or often introductory turns of phrase whereby a speaker indicates what kind of thinking or response he has passed through himself, or identifies in others (his colleagues, or his opponents), or what kind he wishes to call for in his hearers. Certain continuities or similarities may easily enough be traced over the whole of the hundred years or so under review here. Naturally enough, for example, politicians are always inclined to stress how the problems that they deal with call for rational thought. Gladstone once called for 'thorough, searching, impartial and dispassionate enquiry' (16 March 1892). James Callaghan, on 7 March 1979, used the words, 'I should wish to see the possibility examined with care.' Roy Jenkins spoke of the need to 'look objectively at the facts and see which reasoned conclusions...can be drawn from them'.[19]

Within such continuities, though, significant or indeed prominent differences appear. This begins to be so when we look at language where the emphasis seems to be more on the mental experience of logical reasoning – its inner quality as life and consciousness – than on the objective and external need for such logical processes in themselves. Here once again, allowance of some kind must be made for the to us unfamiliar language of the earlier speakers. When Sir Stafford Northcote (23 October 1884) spoke of 'a matter which ought to be very carefully and very *candidly* considered', he was using the word 'candid' in a sense which has virtually disappeared from the language; but clearly, what was in his mind came very close to Gladstone's 'enquiry' as he described it above, or to William Summers's reference to men of '*candid* and impartial mind' (23 October 1884).

With the politicians towards the beginnings of the period under review, that sort of emphasis, psychological rather than simply rational or logical, is particularly recurrent. That that is so, cannot but become a sort of nodal point in this discussion. In Lloyd George's celebrated Budget speech of 29 April 1909,[20] the word 'consider' has a key rôle all the time: 'I have...invited the Committee to consider the prospect in front of them'; 'I come now to the consideration of...'; 'it will require very careful consideration': 'I have now to consider'. The same idea is plain elsewhere in Lloyd George's speeches: 'I should like to examine the claim'; 'if he advised them not to throw it out it must have been after careful consideration of all the conditions'; 'party loyalty has overridden their *judgement*'; 'you can hardly realize, without *going into it thoroughly*, how...'[21] Likewise with 'I did not *deem* it advisable', a remark also in the 1909 Budget speech. Alongside these expressions, one may see how Ramsay MacDonald writes in his pamphlet *Labour and the Empire* (1907). Once again, as with Lloyd George, the phrases that recur are such as 'a greater *maturity of consideration*', or 'the considerations that weigh with us', or 'counterbalancing considerations'.

Of course it would be absurd to suggest that later politicians do not 'consider', or that they do not invite their hearers to do so. Yet all the same, their language suggests that they are less conscious of, and also less interested in, what that is like for the individual consciousness than were their predecessors. Their minds have to some extent turned away from what 'consideration' is as a psychological experience; what they do seem sometimes to remain aware of is rather what it is like as an objective, logical sequence. I hope it is possible to say, without becoming in any way politically partisan, that Roy Jenkins refers rather often to the logical side of political thinking. He certainly leaves the impression of a man wishing to take his stand by logic and rationality. But when it is a matter of touching upon the aspect of this which occupies the individual consciousness, Jenkins's language repeatedly strikes one as a little perfunctory. For Jenkins, thinking sometimes seems like a *logical* process, somehow without very much being a *mental* process, a part of conscious life.

Gladstone, one might say, and some of his contemporaries, seem inclined to stress just how much of mental life, of the mind itself at work, is involved in rational thinking. But on the other hand, there is surely something significant in

Jenkins's repeated use of the contemporary catch-phrase 'to look at', for 'to consider' as we find in the earlier politicians: 'we must look in this way at...'; 'we looked equally carefully...we are looking at alternative means'. The suggestion of externality, of a partial loss not of real power for inner thought, but of a ready-to-hand and vivid sense of its innerness, is redoubled in the remarkable phrase, 'I shall *listen* very carefully to everything they have to say but my job is to *look* at...' Here, attending is externalized into listening, in just the same way that examining or considering is externalized into 'looking at'.

It must be said that Jenkins does not represent his full mind or his full quality by such expressions. Elsewhere, he speaks of 'concentrating our thoughts', or of 'convictions ...held at...a profound level', or says – vividly – 'I paused and thought.' But such remarks, though they indeed qualify what has been said, do not negate it; all the more, because Jenkins not infrequently represents 'concentrating our thoughts', in his own case, in noticeably impersonal, externalized terms. In these cases, we encounter expressions like 'the facts lead me to believe'; 'the balance of argument ...leaning against...'; 'I do not deduce from this'; 'I have never seen the slightest contradiction between...'; 'that seems to me...even less defensible in logic or morals'; 'judged on the basis of hard-headed commercial considerations'; 'we shall work on the basis of the facts'. These expressions all come from the later pages of Jenkins's collected *Essays and Speeches*.

Such a quality of interest in political questions is in itself, no doubt, valid; but it is much to the point for the present discussion. Jenkins conducts his thinking in a world of '*data*' (that is, what is given from outside), and of deductions, contradictions, and arguments *pro* and *contra*. It is all perfectly laudable, from the politician's standpoint; but there remains a significant contrast with, for example, some words of Sir Stafford Northcote in the House of Commons on 23 October 1884. It happens that he uses just the same form of words as Jenkins did, in one of the passages quoted above. But immediately, the inner dimension supervenes upon the outer: 'I shall listen to the arguments *and consider the grounds and reasons.*' Here one sees an almost instinctive, unpremeditated stress upon how the external, auditory perception of spoken language transforms itself into individualized inner experience, into thought as it extends perception. Logic integrates itself into a personality; it becomes individual experience. There begins to emerge a likeness with the discussion of Tolstoy on pages 82–5 below; and a certain likeness, also, with the discussion of personality-structures (pages 81–2).

One may say, however, that even Jenkins's political thought has a more Apollonian dimension that that of some other comparatively recent politicians of not dissimilar convictions. Indeed, his speeches taken as a whole leave a somewhat unusual impression of thoughtfulness and the reflective mind, even though they do so within the limits that have been outlined above. Herbert Morrison's *The Peaceful Revolution* (1949) leaves another impression: that he may sometimes have tried to accommodate his hearers on easy terms, as it were, by choosing language that suggested how political thinking could be effortless, simple and trouble-free. I have added the italics in the passages which follow, in order to emphasize what seems to create this impression. 'If we *go away with a picture in our minds*' (that was not said in condemnation of such a response, but the reverse); 'let us *keep that picture in mind*'; 'I will try to *give you some idea*'; 'it seems to me time we all *did a bit more thinking*'; it is 'the British way to *tend to feel* that...'; 'they are satisfied that *we know what time of day it is*'.

Sometimes, admittedly, it seems that Morrison was speaking in another and more inward vein; and occasionally that is true. At one point, for example, he speaks of the need 'to match the new legislation with a new spirit'. On the other hand, though, what seems like a greater inwardness can suddenly dissolve and prove not to have been there. We read, for example, of 'a great change in the whole heart, mind and spirit of the Labour Party'. But Morrison goes on, almost at once, to explain those words in terms which, from the standpoint of this present discussion, render them nugatory:

'there had been a considerable degree of modernization...of political realism, of *improvement in its* [that is, the Labour Party's] *publicity techniques'*. Likewise, there is one point at which Morrison begins to speak of the importance of individuality. But it soon proves to be the case that the word 'individual' is being used only in a metaphorical sense. Morrison's point is simply that local authorities are not all alike in their wishes or methods, and that it is a good thing for them to maintain their 'individuality' in that figurative sense. Similarly he speaks of how 'electoral agents have to understand humanity'. That remark is transformed, and surely loses its inwardness, with the words that immediately follow: '...understand humanity *and how to handle it'*. If humanity is a thing to 'handle', one is not much concerned with its Apollonian potentialities.

Those words of Morrison's perhaps go aptly with one of Harold Wilson's not-very-frequent references (*Purpose in Power*, p. 28) to 'individuals'. But all that transpires, at that point in his remarks, is that individuals can now sue the Crown. It is somewhat similar with a reference made by Wilson to 'our deep reserves of understanding and concern' (p. 14). These deep reserves are as far from individualization as it is possible for them to be, since they are the reserves of the whole nation envisaged *collectively*. That such expressions seem to turn up more easily in a metaphorical use about a collective body, than literally and with reference to the speaker or his hearers or indeed anyone else individually considered, is food for thought in itself. Expressions in Attlee's speeches sometimes have rather the same ring about them. 'The moral sense of *mankind* – a sense of the corporate interests of *the human race'*; 'the deep feelings of *all the peoples'* (*Purpose and Policy*, 1947, pp. 106, 120). One begins, even, to ask oneself whether there is some mysterious process whereby a conception of individual life flourishes as a metaphor, at the moment when it is beginning to pass from view in the literal sense.

It will be said, perhaps, that politics is concerned with general principles or with practical possibilities; and that the richness or otherwise of the life of the mind is barely, or only most indirectly, its concern. That may well be true; but the fact remains that earlier politicians wrote and spoke with what appears like a recurrent sense that political thinking called for more than logic operating on fact. Constantly, they refer to some wider and less tangible power of *insight*: as if that were inescapably called for in dealing with the problems that they made their province. Keir Hardie, in *From Serfdom to Socialism* (1907), spoke of the political thinker as an 'earnest seeker after truth', and of a 'living recognition' of the truths of politics. His praise for the conditions of work of the craftsmen of earlier times stresses that under the conditions in which they lived, the tendency had been to 'develop *individuality*'; and he contrasted that with 'modern workshop conditions', which 'are not conducive to the production of either intellect or individuality'. Hardie's criticism of Herbert Spencer's individualistic theory was not at all that it upheld a false ideal, but simply that it 'presupposes certain conditions which do not exist'. Individuality in Spencer's world was individuality only for some; that is what is wrong with it.

Ramsay MacDonald's early *Labour and the Empire* is a document remarkable for its stress upon the less tangible and rational dimensions, and at the same time the more intuitive and individual dimensions, of political awareness. 'Liberalism was becoming confused as though a mist had fallen on its *vision*' (p. 13). In fact, the word 'vision' is characteristic of this essay as a whole: one in which a recurrent and key expression is 'spirit' ('the more sober commercial spirit', p. 5; 'the spirit of nationality', p. 24; 'the democratic spirit', p. 35; 'the political spirit', p. 36). Another key word in the essay is 'imagination' and its derivatives. All the time, the reader finds himself encountering remarks like 'the unimaginative and unsympathetic way it approached foreign politics' (p. 14); 'the lack of imagination which must always make Imperialism a danger' (p. 16); 'when more imaginative and sympathetic rivals appear' (p. 18); 'The British manufacturer...with his fatal lack of imagination' (p. 19); 'these sons of the well-to-do...the least imaginative and sympathetic of men' (p. 26).

There is no need to pursue the point further. One see that

for Ramsay MacDonald, imagination and sympathy had to some extent become clichés; but that affords only confirmation of the view that the clichés of today are different. Alongside these words of Ramsay MacDonald, it is to the point to notice Harold Wilson's call (*Purpose in Power*, p. 81) to succumb to 'no fanciful imaginary picture', and his passing rejection (p. 101) of 'the visionary point of view'. Needless to say, we are dealing in relatives, and on one occasion (p. 79) Wilson speaks of a '*vision* of freedom...[a] conception of life and its possibilities', rather as Attlee once said (*Purpose and Policy*, p. 111) 'I have seen great changes of *conception.*'

Ramsay MacDonald's essay cannot be said to bear the signs of absolutely first-class work; but rather, on the whole, of a thoughtful, humane, inventive, but perhaps also limited mind. Again though, that does not affect the point at issue; and it may be added that, in general, the speeches and writings of the politicians of today, studied after an interval of time, scarcely leave an impression of dazzling distinction.

Hardie's stress on the words 'vision' and 'imagination' may be compared with Lloyd George's emphatic assertion that there is 'nothing more fatal' for a political movement than to 'narrow its vision to the material needs', and that the power of 'imagination' would 'exalt its vision' (*The Great Conspiracy*, p. 25). By the same token, Ramsay MacDonald's constant movement towards a wide and receptive frame of mind, one responsive to the less tangible dimensions of politics, may also easily be matched from the speeches or writings of other politicians of the same period. Lloyd George, in fact, is fond of that very word, 'wide': 'I must invite hon Members to join me in taking a wider survey'; 'a State can and ought to take a longer view and a wider view of its investments than individuals...a State keeps many ledgers, not all in ink' (1909). Elsewhere, Lloyd George uses expressions like 'subtle human considerations' (*Through Terror to Triumph*, p. 22). Another word for which he had a predilection was 'sagacious': 'wisdom, sagacity and foresight': 'sagacious, shrewd, showing deep insight' *The Great Conspiracy*, pp. 6, 33).

Lloyd George's 'longer view and a wider view' was in fact

simply a variation upon Sir Stafford Northcote's pleonastic words in the House of Commons twenty-five years earlier: 'I saw with pleasure that her Majesty had been advised on this occasion to *take a wider and broader* view' (23 October 1884). Yet, if the detail of the diction is pleonastic, the speaker's attempt to identify a kind of inner life and thinking which is other than rigid logical process, and more humane and fuller of insight than that, is still there. The same concern manifests itself in Keir Hardie's *From Serfdom to Socialism*, in language like 'a *feeling of solidarity* is growing inside the [trade union] movement', or 'the socialist *spirit*' or 'a *living* recognition'. The same is true of Ramsay MacDonald sometimes, as when he writes, 'it would express the spirit of the Empire', or 'the growth of a spirit and method appropriate to it', or 'the Colonies will *extend their views*'. Such language, in the mouths of politicians of today or of the recent past, is unusual. One example, perhaps, comes from Herbert Morrison: 'we have a great vision of science in the service of the people. I ask you to share that vision' (*The Peaceful Revolution*, p. 77). Yet it may be said that in those very words, Morrison is displaying his distance from the earlier orators rather than his nearness to them. What a broad, sweeping, ready-to-hand phrase like 'great vision' fails to do is, precisely, to convey that sense of an attempt to identify a 'distinctive kind of inner life', which was the phrase brought to mind by the less bold and sweeping, but more evocative language of Hardie, MacDonald and others.

Few politicians, doubtless, as few other people, are ever going to say that sagacity is bad, imagination superfluous, or the wider view unnecessary. But it remains the case that the Hansard of today, and the collected speeches of contemporary politicians, when they seem to come nearest to having such things in mind, wear a different appearance from that of the politicians of the past. This is not invariably so: 'I should wish to see the possibility examined with care' (Callaghan, 7 March 1979); 'We must look carefully at what is involved' (Tam Dalyell, 17 March 1980); 'I feel that it should be given close consideration' (Arthur Davidson, 23 February 1979); 'how many people have considered...?'

(Morrison, *The Peaceful Revolution*, p. 19); 'the point raised by the right hon Lady is a reasonable one' (Michael Foot, 7 March 1979). But in the second of those passages, one notices the 'look at' phrase, which has been commented upon already; and in the third, the use of the word 'feel' (to indicate an opinion held on the basis of something other than mechanical, cut-and-dried thinking), though common usage today, still points towards a tendency to employ terms of emotion or sentiment to do duty for thinking in that 'wider and broader spirit' with which this discussion has been concerned. That, in fact, is a remarkably widespread tendency in recent political prose – a movement away from the Apollonian, towards, one might say, a simplified and rudimentary Dionysiac. 'This House was *out of sympathy* with a move... to reform' (Leo Abse, 23 February 1979); 'we appreciate the *depth of feeling* associated with them' (William Hamilton); 'a more open and *full-hearted* manner' (Nicholas Winterton); 'those who *feel instinctively*' (Alexander Fletcher, 17 March 1980); 'the Government do not *feel it right* to...' (Morrison, *The Peaceful Revolution*, p. 133); 'of course we are all *disturbed* about this' (Wilson, 9 November 1965); Churchill could 'make each one *feel just that much greater*' (Wilson, 25 June 1965); 'a most *heart-rending* decision' (Eldon Griffiths, 17 March 1980); 'we are *very worried* about the Government's ambivalence'; 'I should be *even more worried*' (Wilson, *Purpose in Politics*, pp. 127, 120); 'we will view it with *very great anxiety indeed*' (Wilson, p. 176). Finally we may consider two examples of language of this kind from Jenkins, who often enough (as has been seen) inclines another way: 'What is *in our mind in looking at* this project', and 'we are *concerned* about' (2 February 1966).

The relative vagueness of both those last phrases affords a kind of bridge to an almost opposite tendency in the political language of the recent past; but it seems to be another way in which the range and fullness of the individual consciousness may remove from the central place. This is a tendency to speak of the complexities and indefinites that can call for the 'wider view', and so forth, in language which is not internalized but externalized: to refer to the complexity of the facts, and not to the complexity of what the mind has to do to comprehend them. One may see the distinction clearly enough, sometimes, in Herbert Morrison. Sometimes Morrison uses a relatively inward kind of language, as when he speaks of the need 'to match the new legislation with a *new spirit*' (*The Peaceful Revolution*, p. 45). Elsewhere he says, 'there was lacking that *overall conception* of the national need' (p. 37). But when he refers to the need 'to keep the *total situation* in mind' (p. 70), one sees the more external kind of reference; and the phrase 'the spirit of understanding *and realism*' (p. 49) neatly straddles the inward and the more externalized modes of expression. Harold Wilson, in his self-evidently sincere and carefully considered speech in the Commons commemorating the death of Churchill, provides another illustration of a tendency to describe the subtler workings of the mind in somehow externalized language: 'he could see the events he was shaping *through the eye of history*' (25 January 1965). It is in no way to dispute or to disparage what Wilson said, to notice the kind of diction that appears to have come to him most naturally and readily at a moment when he was deeply engaged. He did not try to search the depth of Churchill's mind, but rather to see those depths as they were reflected on the surface of outer events.

Perhaps it is rather the same with Jenkins's striking words at the London Labour Party Conference of 1967: 'The core of the problem is to give the party and the nation a clear sense of direction: a *lifting of the sights*, a view, at once sharp and far-reaching, of where we want to get' (*Essays and Speeches*, p. 280). Those words certainly indicate, more clearly than any other that I have encountered in the political language of the recent past, the wish to delineate a richer and wider state of consciousness; the fact that they speak not of the power of 'vision', but of the aids to vision or the objects of it, and turn out immediately to delineate inner consciousness by the means of delineating an external panoramic reality, is striking. Along similar lines are Jenkins's call to '*do a searching but reasonably rapid job*' (*Essays and Speeches*, p. 237); and Davidson's memorable 'we would require *a massive carpentry job* – to use an inelegant phrase – if the Bill went to Committee' (23 February 1979).

This has been a brief and exploratory examination of the matter in hand; and to form opinions about the mode and nature of men's thinking by considering, over a span as long as a hundred years, the language they use simply as they introduce the substance of what they have to say, is perhaps precarious and doubtless inconclusive. Nevertheless, it seems to afford reason for thinking that, to a significant extent, the language of politics has reflected something of the general change which this book tries to trace. That is, a change tending to mutate awareness of the range and depth of the thinking individual's consciousness into a concern rather with what is of an emotional nature simply; or with externalities; or with some kind of inter-subjective, collective reality. It would over-simplify matters to identify this, in respect of political language, with something like an increase in sonorous vagueness. Possibly there has been that; but it is not the point at issue. Sonorous vagueness – or vacuity – has been part of politics for longer than the period that has been surveyed here.

IV 'WORDS, WORDS...'

To discuss language in any way is always an intricate task, and to examine certain features of current and recent English slang and colloquial language will not bring us to any sweeping, hard-and-fast conclusions. This ought to be borne in mind all the time. What also needs to be borne in mind is that the present discussion is not intended to turn upon what commonly preoccupies discussion of the condition of the English language today; but to turn upon the central problem of this book.

Works like H. W. Fowler's *Modern English Usage* (first edition, 1926), or Sir Ernest Gower's *The Complete Plain Words* (1954), concerned themselves very much with whether the English language was being used well or not; and if not, what was wrong and how it should be remedied. Kenneth Hudson's *Dictionary of Diseased English* (1977) is a much later book that focusses upon the same problem, and makes that fact clear in its very title. Many will see what will be said in this present chapter as casting light upon such matters; and they may be right. The intention, however, is to pursue something else. This is, to consider so far as possible what activities of consciousness seem to be called for, or called out, by this or that kind of usage. What must have been going on in the mind of those who coined certain usages, and of those who heard them and understood them when they were first used? (Doubtless the answers to these questions change, as new expressions become familiar, and then second nature, and then worn out and discarded.) Answers to these questions will not necessarily imply anything about using the language well or badly, though some may, until they reflect, think the contrary.

But it is possible to put the question in over-ambitious terms. If it is taken generally, as if it were asking what goes on in the mind of user or hearer, when a word or expression is used intelligently or heard and understood, it becomes a question that philosophers have discussed perennially and with dubious success. There is no need, however, to enter into such profound matters. One may take as a *datum* whatever of consciousness and mental life is involved in, as it were, the 'standard case' of usage or comprehension. The problem here is simply whether, and how, certain special kinds of usage turn out to be modifications of the 'standard case', involving user or hearer (in this discussion, 'hearer' will mean either hearer or reader) in more of mental life and consciousness – or conceivably, less – than that 'standard case'.

It is easy to see that deviations from the 'standard case' of comprehending a word or expression are common and familiar. Whenever, for example, a pun is introduced or the force of it is taken, something occurs which is different from what occurs when a word is used or grasped in a simple sense. If that were not so, the presence of the pun would simply remain unrecognized. Likewise when anyone coins a metaphor and uses it: if there were nothing distinctive in that use, or in taking the point of it, the term in question would simply be understood as it is understood when it is used literally. Such features of language are both familiar and perennial. We can see their truth quite regardless of any study of the distinctively current use of any language – either its slang and colloquialisms, or its newly invented jargon vocabularies.

Certain forms of current or recent English slang, however, make the point particularly clear. This is so with back slang, and with rhyming slang. Self-evidently, these sub-languages, as perhaps they might be termed, call for clearly identifiable extra mental operations on the part of those who use them. Initially at least, the hearer of, say, the term *naf* has to recall that back slang is in use, and secondly has to invert the phonetic sequence of what he hears in order to get the word which he can understand along the lines of the 'standard case'. Likewise with a rhyming slang term like, say, *titfer*: the hearer must become aware that he is being invited to share rhyming slang with the speaker; secondly he must recall that *titfer* is used, in that diction, as short for *tit for tat*; and thirdly he must perform some sort of rhyming operation in order to pass from that, to the word 'hat'. Needless to say, in the course of time, back slang or rhyming slang expressions become so familiar to those who use them that all those processes can atrophy and disappear. But that is beside the point; because the terms would never have been introduced at all, if those extra movements of thought had not, initially, been both necessary and also actually wanted for one reason or another (perhaps for concealment, perhaps to sustain a sense of belonging to some 'in-group', perhaps simply for amusement and jocularity).

I shall say no more of back slang and rhyming slang, because they have not been, and certainly are not now, any general part of colloquial English usage. They make the point, though, about the standard case and deviations from it, particularly clear. Not all slang expressions are in fact deviations from that standard case, even if they were so once in the past. Many slang or colloquial expressions function in our language like ordinary words used literally. They cannot be joyfully unravelled as one hears them – though they could once, no doubt – and have to be learnt by users just as standard-English words are learnt. Certainly they have a derivation, an etymology, but it is no more part of their current usage than is the etymology of a standard-English word. *Hip*, as in 'hippies', appears to come from *hep*, and that from the ploughman's call to his horses ('Hup!') telling them to get up and be lively. *Chuffed* (gratified) comes from a dialect word *chuff* meaning 'happy', and *chocker* is originally a naval term related to the condition of a pulley-block when it can provide no further purchase. *Dekko* (a look, a glance) came into vagrants' slang in the nineteenth century from Romany; and again, apparently independently and a good deal later, into army slang from Hindustani.[22] But in none of these cases do users of the words use them with any sense, any more, of the ploughman's call, the dialect word, the pulley-block, or the background in Romany or Hindustani. All of them function in English slang as what one might call 'quasi-roots'. The mental activity, the mode of consciousness, involved in selecting, using, or comprehending them is surely no different from what it is with any word used in its basic and literal sense. They are examples of the 'standard case'.

Likewise with three low expressions which are current for the female sexual organ. According to Partridge, one of these may be connected with the Spanish verb *quemar*, to burn. A second is elegantly if discreetly adverted to, I believe, by T. S. Eliot in *The Waste Land*: after bowdlerizing the Australian ballad about 'Mrs Porter and her daughter', and how (and where) they wash themselves, he drops us a hint or half-hint in the nightingale's 'Twit twit twit' which follows immediately. Partridge relates this word to obscure words meaning 'a passage', or 'to mend a gap in a hedge'. The third such expression he relates to an Old English word for the womb. But today, none of these three words re-activates, for the generality of users or hearers, any part whatsoever of all that.

It is rather to the point, however, that today only the third of those three expressions seems to be widely used (not, doubtless, in polite conversation); and moreover, that no other expressions seem to be available to speakers save the appropriate medical terms. It is at this point that a certain contrast begins to appear, between the slang of recent years or today, and that of, say, eighty or a hundred years ago. If we go back that far, we find a remarkably wide variety of available expressions, and moreover we recognize that many of them, if they were to be selected knowingly and comprehended properly, unmistakably called for what has to be regarded as an expansion of consciousness and mental activity. Thus *masterpiece*, which became obsolete early this century, is an appropriate term for the object in question, only because speakers and hearers could recognize an apt catachresis from, say, the use of that word for works of art. Moreover, the term had little point unless they also recalled, momentarily, why that part of a woman's body deserved to be praised so highly; and further again, some of the point is lost unless one sees that the expression can also mean 'piece belonging to, or the special concern of, the master'. The fact that *masterpiece* was current slang when *piece* was itself 'low colloquial' for a woman 'especially sexually', is also to the point. To use the word in this way meant activating some or all of these additional reverberations.

It cannot be said that those suggestions are mere pointless ingenuity, and that for an obvious reason. *Masterpiece* must have remained current, in this low sense, for two centuries, because it made some genuine contribution to what used to be called 'the talk'. It enabled speakers and hearers to identify and relish its overtones and suggestions, its appositeness and wit. As a mere vacuous, superfluous synonym, it would have served no purpose except to mystify or bore, and it would have gone. Likewise with *seminary* ('mid-nineteenth to twentieth centuries: obsolete'): there is a double pun on 'semen' and on the learning establishment, and presumably a lively recognition of how different are the things to be learnt in this 'seminary' from what is learnt in the other ones. Likewise with *ace of spades*, which is pointless unless the visual appearance and also I suppose the unbeatable value of aces generally, are recalled. *Parsley-bed* relates to visual appearance and also to why introducing the word 'bed' is ingeniously apt. *Mustard-pot* embodies among other things a reference to how expressions like *burnt, fireship* and *fire-plug* used to have associations with venereal disease. *Mangle, shaving-brush, melting-pot, Mount Pleasant* (an old Inner London suburb), *front parlour, muff, ladder* and *mousetrap* need no comment. All of them called upon users and hearers to engage in additional mental operations, to elaborate their consciousness momentarily; and all are recorded by Partridge as obsolete.

Some of the low expressions for the male sexual organ formed witty pairs with those for the female. *Silent flute* paired with *silent beard, mole* with *mole-catcher, pen* with *pen-wiper, needle* with *needle-case* and *pestle* with *mortar*. Other terms also invited and made possible an expansion of thought into their implications and aptness. *Pilgrim's staff* made one think, I suppose, of how the pilgrim depended on his staff to get him through the trials of life; *bald-headed hermit* that a hermit would spend most of his life in isolation and solitude, but not quite all of it no doubt. *Nimrod* is the mighty hunter; *lullaby*, which Partridge notes as 'mid-nineteenth to twentieth century' and queries as obsolete, is food for thought in more ways than one.

Virtually all of those expressions are obsolete today. All invited those who used or heard them to do so with a consciousness awakened to some wealth or multiplicity of meaning, and most of them advertised their sensuous vividness, whether visual or kinaesthetic. Another class of expression for the same things may be identified, however, and will prove particularly interesting later. *Commodity* (female) and *credentials* (male) are examples. These have a new kind of aptness, but one which is still 'food for thought'. If one puts one's mind to some extent back into earlier ways of thought, one can see that the former was a principle thing that a woman had to offer, and the latter was what especially established a man's worth. *Premises* (female) has its obvious aptness too. But the aptness is part only of the story, and in fact it seems as it two further points ought to be made.

First, all three of those words came from commerce or the law, and part of their effectiveness was how their use established, as between speakers and hearers, a common ground of experience that was not only sexual. Second, though, speakers and hearers must have been sufficiently *au fait* to use terms that on the face of it seem conspicuously generic and abstract – precisely because, with their detailed common knowledge and understanding and experience, they could be given perfectly specific meanings by all. The joke was that the conversation pretended to be dry and generic, while the mind could fill with, and savour, how that was not so at all. Likewise with calling a girl an *article* or a mistress a *peculiar* (in the older sense of that word, meaning something 'distinctively personal' to someone). With that, one may compare *particular*, either in the same sense, or more generally for one's favourite drink, blend of tea, etc. In each case, the details were familiar and vivid enough for a special pleasure to be taken in calling them out by an expression chosen for its abstract nature, and from quite another sphere of life. *Monosyllable* is a rather similar example: ostensibly quite undefined, the wit lies in how that is not so at all.

Possibly it will be a surprise to some readers to encounter this plenitude of metaphor, second meanings, punning and humour (weak no doubt, some of it) by comparison with the somewhat bleak dearth of terms, whether low or clinical, in use today. It may be thought that that is a mark of our greater honesty and directness in such matters at the present time: we do not require, and should not enjoy, a plethora of tedious euphemisms, because we do not jib at speaking openly of the thing itself. Possibly: but it has no bearing on the state of the language, in this particular area, that such lack of inhibition may have caused or facilitated, or on the kind and volume of mental activity that using it brings about. Likewise one may compare the current bleak 'to have sex' with to *give hard for soft*, or *horizontal refreshment* or *blanket hornpipe* (from c. 1810: 'obsolete'), or *bread-and-butter fashion*, or *knee-trembler*, or *to make a dog's match of it* (love-making standing up, or by the roadside). Or again, there is *mule* for a sexually impotent man, *pullet-squeezer* for 'a womanizer who "likes 'em young"', *pastry* for pretty young women, the *baby's public house* for a woman's breasts, or – to take a wider view of these matters – the *iron parenthesis* for prison, a *pair of compasses* for a man's legs, *in morocco* for naked, *bosom friend* for a body-louse, *ancient mariners* for Oxford or Cambridge dons who made up a rowing eight, or *put to bed with a shovel* for bury. Many of those obsolete expressions and phrases referred to things we might still commonly wish to refer to, and have no inhibitions over speaking directly about. But Victorian slang and colloquialism had a kind of Shakespearean plenitude. To speak it or follow it was more than communication, it was a complex elaboration of life.

It would of course be absurd to suggest that slang or low language today contains no vivid expressions, expressions which can be turned over joyfully in the mind and become 'food for thought'. Quite often, though, such expressions originally belonged, and have remained, peculiar to some distinctive walk of life, often the armed forces. To *get one's feet under the table* was Second World War army slang for finding a hospitable civilian household. *Lightning-conductors* are naval full-dress trousers with gold stripes down the seams, and *station-master's hat* is naval officers' slang for caps with gilt peaks as worn by senior officers. *G-string* is now the term for the one exiguous garment sometimes worn by strip-tease dancers, but originated in Japanese prisoner-of-war camps as a term for a loin-cloth. *Chinese gunpowder* is current hauliers' slang for cement (i.e., it sticks together instead of exploding). We have *cat's eyes* on our major roads, and in Citizens' Band radio jargon (originating with American lorry-drivers) a tyre is a *doughnut*, a policeman is a *bear*, and a woman police patrol is a *honey bear*. *Rat race*, coined about 1945, *one-armed bandit*, coined in the late 1950s for a gambling-machine, and *in the doghouse*, also from the 1950s, all illustrate how there are certainly vivid and thought-provoking slang expressions that have been coined in the recent past.

Yet a general review of current slang suggests that such expressions are hardly typical. What seems to be more so are expressions and turns of phrase which have a certain clipped, minimal quality, as if they were intended not to 'say more' (making their point more richly and vividly or wittily than standard English might do) but to make it in a somewhat flat style, leaving the impression of as little expenditure of linguistic or mental energy as possible. Perhaps it should again be said, it does not follow that that is a criticism.

The most obvious way in which this seems to show, is the degree to which current slang exploits the shortest, plainest, in a sense emptiest words in the language. The frequency of the word *it* makes an illustration; and while of course this manifests a perennial resource of the language, the point is how such usages predominate, and how there are not, today, contrasting kinds of usage available as much as in the not distant past. *It* not only means either the male or female sexual organ (from the nineteenth century), and something like sexual appeal (early twentieth century), but occurs in a variety of expressions like *you're for it, with it, you've had it*. These usages contrast with some noted earlier on. They do not employ the vague word *it* so that users and hearers may come together in the pleasure of covertly identifying its meaning exactly; but they employ it specifically for its no-trouble vagueness. Also, those very phrases illustrate two other prominent linguistic features of current slang: reliance on minimal adverbs or prepositions (sometimes these are not altogether easy to distinguish), and reliance on the commonest and in a sense 'flattest' of English verbs.

Along these lines we encounter phrases like *the in thing, it turns me on*, stockings are *out*, a *hang-up*, a *get-out*, a *pushover, not on*, the *low-down*, a *drop-out, way out*, a *sit-in*, and even a *be-in* (a gathering for the sake simply of company). The point about nearly all of those phrases is that (as before with *it*) the adverbial part of the expression remains as vague as it can possibly be, and that that is part of the intention. These expressions work quite differently from 'credentials' and so on, where it was a kind of joke that what could be identified exactly could be spoken of periphrastically.

There is also a large class of colloquial or slang phrases utilizing a small group of very common English verbs which, because of the multiplicity of expressions into which they have long entered, have very unspecific and general meanings. These phrases take a verb-plus-adverb form: in Citizens' Band lingo, to *bring it on* is to accelerate, to slow down is to *let off*. Among the most important verbs of this kind are *come, do, get, have, make, put* and *take*. They produce expressions like *come again!* (repeat what you said), *come-on, come-back, come it* (give oneself airs), *come off it* (cease to exaggerate: characteristically perhaps, the original nineteenth-century form of this, 'Come off *the grass!*' has been truncated), *come and get it* (army slang for 'the meal is ready'), *come clean*, or *come-hither* used as an adjective. *Do* of course has the meaning, as a noun, of 'entertainment' or 'function' (from c. 1930) as well as other significations. As a verb, *do* has entered over centuries into many colloquial expressions; but the twentieth century *she does things to me* is worthy of note. *Get* occurs, recently, in *get the message, get across* (either 'to communicate successfully' or 'to irritate'), *get it* (be wounded), *get with it, get a load of this, get cracking, get weaving, get off with* (from c. 1940 or perhaps earlier), a *get-out*, or to *get stuck into it*. *Have* as noun means a fraud or disappointment, and occurs also in phrases like *have had it* (c. 1939), *have it away together* (c. 1950), and *have it off* (c. 1940). Since about 1918, *make* has meant to have intercourse with a woman, and there is also to *make it* (succeed: c. 1933), to *make it together* (late 1940s), to *make the county* (be accepted in county society: c. 1945), *makes you think, doesn't it?* (c. 1939), *on the make* (c. 1920), and *make up* in the sense of 'promote'. Partridge notes this sense as 'c. 1925' and relates it to the promotion of army NCOs and how they become more 'painted and powdered' with badges, etc.; but it is also used in business circles. *Put* gives a *put-on* (hoax), to *put down* (land: c. 1916, and to employ artillery fire, 1939–45), and *put it on* ('show off', from the late nineteenth century). *Take* gives *take off* ('go away': c. 1945), *take a dim view of* (c. 1937), *take you up on it, take it* (endure rough usage), *take it out of* (make tired), *take it out on* (vent frustration), and the conspicuously minimal to *have what it takes* (c. 1935). Other examples of similarly constructed expressions, with rather less common verbs, are *fill me in* (supply information: early 1940s), *pack it in* (desist: c. 1925), *pack up* (cease to function: c. 1937), or *fall down on* (fail: c. 1935).

To list, and doubtless also to read, all these slight-seeming slang or colloquial expressions of recent times is laborious; but the point about them is not really made, unless one sees how common they have become and how readily they are used. In almost every case, moreover, there is no element of wit, punning or metaphor; and in the few of which that cannot be said (*take a dim view, pack up*), the metaphorical sense is either not clearly identifiable, or – it seems fair to say – makes only a minimal contribution.

Such usages may indeed not be inferior or manifest a decline in the language. Both those relying on the semantic versatility of English adverbs and prepositions, and those relying on the versatility of the commonest English verbs, conform much to the perennial nature and strength of English. They function, on the whole, somewhat like the quasi-roots discussed at the beginning of this chapter. Each must be learnt separately (one cannot deduce the meaning of *make up* as above, say, from *make it* or *make out*); and once learnt, all they require is that basic element of consciousness required for what was called above the 'standard case' of using a meaningful expression. What they do not do is to invite the mind to explore and savour a fuller semantic expanse: like the ingenious catachresis, the punning, the metaphorical life which characterized many earlier colloquial expressions. What commends these more recent phrases is their idiomatic brevity, and their quality exactly of not requiring effort in order to unravel ingenuity. They are labour-saving English and also 'cool' English. They display how users prefer equanimity to extra effort. There has been some tendency for slang and colloquial language to change in function; from words for amusement and interest, inviting the consciousness of user or hearer to reflect or explore or enjoy, to words for utility and convenience.

That same tendency towards the minimal and utilitarian can be seen, linguistically, in other respects. On of these has shown itself in a phrase like 'the in *thing*', cited already. Now, however, it is the noun rather than the preposition which is to the point; and one recalls other phrases like *to have a thing about* (obsession, phobia: c. 1935), *a fun thing, do one's own thing, the done thing, just one of those things* (c. 1936), or the wide variety of slightly technical or specialist expressions, though used only in conversation, like *this geographical distribution thing. Thing* has of course entered into colloquial expressions before the present century, but that is beside the point. *Job* is another word, of the same minimal semantic kind, that has proliferated in recent colloquialisms. *Just the job* (c. 1935), a *blonde (brown, wizard) job* (c. 1940), a *jet job* (fast car: Canadian, c. 1948). From our politicians we have already encountered 'a massive carpentry job', and 'a searching but reasonably rapid job' (see above, pp. 52–3). *Bit* has long been a similar word: among more recent developments are to *have a bit* or *a bit of the other* (intercourse: late ninteenth century, c. 1930), a *bit of all right* (twentieth century), *bit of homework* (late nineteenth century) and *bit of skirt* (Australian: c. 1900). *Date* (the person with whom one has a date: c. 1944) is similar; so is '*hot stuff*' (twentieth century), '*book of words*' (instructions: twentieth century), and 'in a big *way*' (c. 1935). *Happening*, too recent for Partridge presumably, is another example.

Words like *thing, job, bit* and so on, open up a new area of this whole subject. One way in which to see how this is so is to consider the word 'affair'. That word has meant the genitals since the nineteenth century, it appears; but also, from c. 1800, Partridge records it as a colloquialism for things like buildings or machines – a usage which he then describes as *becoming standard English*. The point is, that the tendency towards free and frequent use of semantically minimal generic words seems increasingly to have become a feature of English in contexts which cannot be thought of as colloquial.

One example is the word *case*, though not only in a colloquial expression like *a hard case*, which Partridge records as imported from the United States, c. 1860. Fowler wrote, in *Modern English Usage*, 'There is perhaps no single word so freely resorted to *as a trouble-saver*' (italics mine), and we have seen that saving trouble has become something of a feature of current English. If *case* functions that way, that is because of how its meaning is generic and undetermined. Among Fowler's examples (and condemned by him, though again that is not the point here) are: 'In the case of *Pericles*, the play is omitted', and the memorable 'In the case of no poet is there less difference between the poetry of his youth and that of his later years.'

Fowler does not enter *situation* in the first edition of his book, but by 1977, Kenneth Hudson records expressions in business advertisements like 'the manufacturing *situation*', 'people in work *situations*' and 'management *situation*': the first two are from advertisements in *The Times*, the third from one in *New Society*. These usages are quite different from those of *commodity* or *credentials* discussed earlier. A manufacturing situation is in no way some very specific thing which user and hearer can identify specifically while they derive relish and amusement from referring to it generically. It is genuinely, and necessarily, a vague thing, and the intention – naturally enough, in an advertisement – is to leave it so. *Relationship* is another word of the same kind; as everyone knows, today it is used freely of the deepest and most intimate bonds between people. Other words of this type are *environment* ('a progressive working environment': advertisement in *The Daily Telegraph*, 28 September 1982), *experience* (Hudson quotes 'a candle-lit dining experience'), *event*, *gap* (generation, credibility gap), *phase* ('you will always get a lag phase', I heard recently) *paradigm* (Hudson quotes 'Here we find ourselves in a new paradigm whose implications have this potential to reap havoc in our universities': *Times Higher Educational Supplement*, 1976), *range* ('in the age range 30 years to 40 years', and 'product ranges', both from advertisements in *The Daily Telegraph*, 28 September 1982: 'price range' has also become common), and perhaps also *strategy* ('innovative strategies', *ibid.*), *systems*, and *scenario*.

There seems no doubt that this style of expression resembles the colloquialisms discussed earlier. The intention, or at least part of the intention, is to make a limited communication in a form which commits one to a minimum, and which evokes a minimal mental response of identifying, discriminating, endorsing or rejecting. That this is a comparatively recent development may be seen at once, if we compare advertisements of a hundred, or indeed fifty years ago, with even one of today:

A steady young person wanted, as useful maid, to attend on a lady and three little girls, out of the nursery. Good needlewoman, dressmaker and milliner. Address, stating wages, to Mrs. Pearson...
(*The Times*, 29 September 1882)

Partner wanted...possessing great business experience and an intimate knowledge of the country and language [of Chile], to carry on business as general merchants. The profits are large and certain.   (*The Times*, 29 September 1882)

Old-established merchants have opening for active director... certified accounts, open to any investigation, show steady and substantial profits over a number of years.
                                (*The Times*, 29 September 1932)

Our client has asked us to locate a first class, career minded PA who is seeking total involvement and challenging position. The chosen applicant will be PA to a top executive in an international entertainment organization, and as such will need to be mature, confident and able to take control when he travels abroad. Good secretarial skills and a fluent European language (French ideal) are needed. CVs will be required.   (*The Times*, 29 November 1982)

Sir Ernest Gowers condemned usage like that quoted above from recent advertisements, and elsewhere, with the words: 'the reason for preferring the concrete to the abstract is clear. Your purpose must be to make your meaning clear'. It was therefore desirable to avoid that 'penumbra of uncertainty' which surrounds all words, but abstract ones more than the others. That account of the writer's purpose may be adequate, or may not. The question may be easier to answer, once certain further features of current or recent usage enter the question.

One of these is an apparent tendency to limit or reduce the total vocabulary which is, so to speak, 'in play' in a given realm of discourse. True, many new specialist fields of work have brought in new words that are more or less 'technical terms'. Yet at the same time, there is an interesting opposite tendency. Thus C. L. Barnhart's *Dictionary of New English, 1963–72* (1973) lists many word coinages that are simply negatives of existing technical terms: *de-restrict, de-escalate, de-bureaucratize, de-criminalize, de-orbit* (to take a missile out of orbit) and *de-pollute*. 'Re-decontamination' has also been recorded elsewhere. Barnhart also notices words like *disbenefit*, and *disemplane* (to leave an aircraft). Examples of the same kind of vocabulary discussed by Hudson include *decrement, de-emphasis, disconfirm, non-imitate, less academic, under-achievement* and *negatively privileged*. The trio of terms in the world of computing, 'hardware' (equipment), 'software' (documents, etc.) and *liveware* (people) is another and memorable example. In certain respects, there seems to be a tendency to multiply technical terms only so far, and then as it were to play variations on them, rather than innovate further.

However much or little one likes such language, the present issue is what kind of mental consciousness and mental activity it requires for its use; and this probably cannot be decided until one sees what purpose it may serve. Clearly it is possible to claim that limiting one's vocabulary in these ways to some degree reduces the mental demands which use of more techical terms, or a mixture of technical terms and standard English, might require. Once *escalate* is in use, a certain further mental effort would be required (by comparison with using *de-escalate*) to identify that a standard English term like *diminish* was its exact contrary. Certainly, extra mental activity would be needed if a second and different technical term (one might suggest *deorsumate*, Lat. *deorsum*, downwards) had to be invented and acquired. Likewise, if the accepted contraries of *emplane*, *benefit* and *confirm* were standard English expressions: *leave*, *harm* and *argue against*, perhaps (there is a difficulty here, because *disconfirm* may perhaps mean 'disprove', or even simply 'fail to confirm'). But in general, those awkward-looking negatives doubtless save a certain degree of mental effort, and that may well be not bad but good.

Probably, however, there is more to be said. There is reason to think that when Gowers wrote 'your purpose must be to make your meaning clear', and said nothing more, his account was a little over-simple. If the specialists were to say 'amount less', 'leave', and 'harm' instead of *decrement*, *disemplane*, and *disbenefit*, they would be put to somewhat more inconvenience than merely the trifling extra mental effort involved in identifying contraries. The extra loss is what actually comes when specialists have to lapse from their technical language into simple standard English that anyone might use. Sustaining the use of technical language is one of the things that all the time helps them, and their readers, who are also specialists or would-be specialists, to sustain a sense of belonging to a distinctive group and pursuing a distinctive common purpose. Of course, such terms sometimes function as what Fowler contemptuously called 'trouble-savers'. But they also function as morale-sustainers; the implications of that for the main question under discussion will have to be considered in a moment. Citizens' Band lingo says *affirmative* and *negatory* for 'yes' and 'no', and nothing could be clearer as indicating a vocabulary that has developed to sustain a sense of belonging, rather than baldly to communicate. One prominent purpose of 'CB-ing', in fact, was originally for long-distance lorry-drivers to have a kind of company as they drove, so that they should not be bored and perhaps fall asleep. Another somewhat curious case came to my notice recently, when the Association of University Teachers announced that it would consider 'taking *industrial* action'. That reads a little strangely, until one recalls that the meaning 'advising its members not to work' is probably less important than enabling all concerned to enjoy the sensation of being in unity with all those who do in fact work in industry.

Probably there is another kind of service, also, that at least some of those ungainly negatives and periphrases could serve. This second element in the case may be seen if words like *under-achievement*, *low-popular*, *less talented*, *de-selected* (dismissed from a training programme) and the like are considered. The English language has, or at least not long ago had, quite another vocabulary for referring to what those words are now used to refer to. That other vocabulary, probably still familiar to all, though out of use, comprises words like *failure*, *flop*, *dunce*, *backward*, *dull*, *dismissed*. But there are strong forces acting on most or all of us, not to use such terms in speech or in writing. There is even, one might say, a sense that so much as to allow oneself to think by means of them is destructive both of the matters in hand, and of one's capacity to think about such matters. Not all evasions of this kind (if that word may pass) can be taken very seriously, of course. The tourist advertisement that spoke of cheaper terms for 'the unhurried months' in Wales (advertisement, *Radio Times*, September 1982) had found a harmless way of not reminding its readers that any part of Wales was actually crowded with visitors at any time in the year. Psychologists who pair off *intra-punitiveness* and *extra-punitiveness* have achieved, among other things, a way of not reminding their readers that some people are destructively aggressive, and as such both dangerous and repellent.

Again, words like *handicapped* or *underprivileged* enable users to avoid the offensiveness, to others and no doubt to themselves also, of words like *crippled, deformed, destitute*, or even *poor*. Fifty years ago and more, those were in common use (so was *poverty-stricken*). It is quite plausible to claim that it is better, not only for the victims of such circumstances, but for everyone, simply not to 'make your meaning clear' every time. Perhaps, indeed, there is even something to be said, along the same lines, for avoiding a word like 'victim'. Trivial examples, but showing the same underlying principle, are *motion discomfort, hygiene hire company* and *soiled*, to avoid speaking of travel sickness, hand-towels, or dirty linen. Recently it has been proposed to drop the medical term *mongol* as 'offensive', and speak of *Down's syndrome* instead.

It seems not improbable that some of the metaphorical expressions which occur in certain areas of language-use today, and at first sight seem to contrast with generic vocabularies like *environment* and the rest, ought to be understood along rather similar lines of 'togetherness'. When we read (the following examples are all from *The Daily Telegraph*, 28 September 1982) 'the position *reports to* the Group Chief Secretary Executive', is part of the contribution of the metaphor to recall earlier memories of days in the armed forces? – or if not that, at least to evoke some sense of belonging to a large, highly-organized, intensely determined body like an army? Expressions like 'innovative *strategies*', or '*in the* cotton/cotton synthetic *field* (in one context, *in the field* means 'on active service') may function similarly: giving a general, diffused sense of some determined and organized solidarity, hinting at a quasi-military world of decisive action, even of heroic achievement. Such overtones and evocations can easily be quite as important, to all concerned, as 'making your meaning clear' in the plain factual sense.

Hudson quotes another startling but apparently not uncommon metaphor from advertising: 'candidates should have a good production *pedigree*'. It is most unlikely that the advertiser wished to consider candidates' forebears, and the metaphor was therefore actively misleading if given its natural meaning. That natural meaning requires, in fact, to be shut off. It looks as if the main contribution of *pedigree* would be to convey a sense that the successful candidate for the job will find himself within a world where affluent pursuits like horse-breeding are familiar topics.

Likewise perhaps with 'our *well-bred* collection of sheets...and pillow-cases', also quoted by Hudson. That phrase may appeal, of course, also to a wider kind of social snobbery or the like. Another example is 'the *hard-nosed* fields of management or science', which Hudson gives as another example, not apparently from an advertisement. That metaphor also implies familiarity with stock-breeding: bulls are 'hard-nosed' when they tend to ignore guidance from those in charge of them – the metaphor simply cannot be applied in its natural sense, or it leads to nonsense. In 'a person with a *track record* that shows senior management potential' (*Daily Telegraph*, 28 September 1982), the metaphor is of more use in conveying that prospective candidates can rest assured they will be entering a world where sport and athletics are lively interests and familiar parlance, than in conveying anything else. A phrase like 'this is a new *ball-game*', probably chiefly American still, may serve the same kind of purpose, helping to establish and sustain a reassuring sense of solidarity between users and hearers, or perhaps sustaining a sense that the matters under discussion are such as may be thought about in an easy, confident frame of mind. Certainly, when a new phase in international politics is called a 'new ball-game', the thought of its seriousness is to some extent blocked off.

Throughout this chapter, the underlying purpose has been, not to assess goodness or badness, but so far as possible to consider what degree and kind of mental life, what activity of consciousness, some of the recent innovations in usage seem likely to have brought. One may reasonably conclude that, despite many new usages that do indeed offer vivid detail or intricate play of language, for the most part our recent linguistic innovations have given prominence to one or other of two things. The first has been the development and strengthening of a clipped, brief, no-trouble kind of language: one which involves a minimum of effort and also does something to convey that the user is sparing of effort and habitually avoids display, effort, intensity, or striving after effect. The implications of that with regard to the 'degree and kind of mental life' that it involves, are clear. The second development is that much current language as used in the more specialized areas of life, including industry, commerce and the professions has, as something prominent among its purposes, to sustain a sense of belonging, or to extrude and shut off unwelcome ideas. In the latter case, that the current usage is promoting not an expansion but a narrowing of consciousness, is obvious. That is integral to the intention. In the former case, it is clear on reflection that the same is true. Here too, we have a kind of minimum-effort language. All the technical terms in a discourse, however long, insofar as this result is part of their contribution, are doing one and the same thing, over and over, from beginning to end. They all serve the one purpose of group reassurance and sense of togetherness. Likewise, the military, horse-breeding and athletic metaphors that seem to get scattered through advertisements for jobs all contribute together, not in any exact and discriminatory way (as if any advertisement would indicate that the firm's ethos was athletic but *not* quasi-military, for example), but to a loose, general sense of energetic affluence. Here too, the limitation of consciousness to the one generalized and diffused impression is clear. Nothing in human affairs is more intricate and varied than language, and no generalization about it can be made to which even striking exceptions cannot be found. But how the findings of the present chapter bear upon the general theme of this book cannot be mistaken.

V 'PERSONOLOGY' PERSONALITIES

THIS CHAPTER will discuss the study of personality by certain social psychologists or sociologists. It will necessarily be selective, and no claim is made that the selection is representative. Nor is such a claim necessary to the argument: which is, that one can see similarities, in these fields of enquiry, to some of the developments and trends discussed in the previous chapters. A similarity is not a fundamental identity: it looks merely as if underlying forces which throw up certain generic similarities may be at work. Part of my purpose is to invite others, better qualified than I, to consider whether this line of thought might be pursued in other fields again.

Undoubtedly there are certain social psychologists whose work strikes a common chord with parts of what emerged, in the first chapter of this book, about twentieth-century art. For them, the individuality of the 'self' lies mainly in its 'spontaneity' (compare p. 20 above). Karen Horney, whose work is more widely known in the United States than in Britain, writes, 'the spontaneous individual self is the spontaneous assertion of one's individual initiative, feelings, wishes, opinions'.[23] In that remark, the order of the words is significant: 'opinions' come last in the list, and even then they seem to be conceived of as being spontaneous like all the rest, not the product of disciplined sequences of thinking. Or again, Karen Horney writes 'the real self is the most alive centre for ourselves', the source of 'spontaneous interests and energies', the 'spring of emotional forces, of constructive energies, of directive and judiciary powers'. This statement is like the other in that again, the words 'directive and judiciary powers' come at the end, and we seem to be encountering opinions in the absence of what properly forms opinions, viz., thinking. Moreover, powers that are directive and judiciary presumably also involve other people, involve interacting membership of a social group. That is why it is fair to link Karen Horney with a more popular-style writer like Carl Rogers, whose *On Personal Power* (1978) seems at first preoccupied with spontaneity, inner integrity, rejection of conventionalizing double-talk and the like, but proves on closer study to see spontaneity in a particular way: as spontaneous *relating to others*. In this mode of thinking, the test, and more, the very status, of the inner is ultimately not itself, but the outer and the social. In a limited sense, certainly, it is true that the outer is the test of the inner. What we can all take into account about the individual and his spontaneity, or anything else in regard to his consciousness, has to be observable from outside. But the dissolution of an existent into its overt symptoms goes much further than just saying that to study that existent requires it to manifest overt symptoms.

When a man of letters turns to the reading of sociology, he is likely to feel an inclination to lay about him on all sides. Some sociologists do not write decent or even lucid English and their statements sometimes end up stating little or nothing. But for all that, much research has been done on aspects of the relation between individual personality on the one hand, and the influence on the individual of other people on the other hand. Often this research is impressive, insofar as it deploys systematic and sophisticated modes of statistical analysis, such as make complaints about style seem a little cheap. But an important qualification must be made to that: it is impossible for refined analysis to yield results which are more refined than the original categories and data to which the analysis is applied.

Consider one example of this kind of work: Frieda Goldman-Eisler's article on 'Breastfeeding and Character Formation' included in *Personality in Nature, Society and Culture* (ed. C. Kluckholm and H. A. Murray, 1948). A hundred adult subjects and also their mothers (mothers appear to have long and exact memories in these matters) were studied, and the basic data subjected to certain sophisticated statistical analyses and corrections. The results offered a good measure of confirmation of the psychoanalytic hypothesis (intrinsically probable, I must add, to the plainest common sense) that stingy breast-feeding and early weaning correlates with a personality inclined to pessimism, passivity, withdrawal, sense of insecurity and so forth: while generous breast-feeding and late weaning go more with being optimistic, active and sociable. The experiment also suggested that psychoanalysts are more correct in linking early weaning with a pessimistic outlook than in linking it with aggression, impatience, and the like: which would be an important additional finding.

However, while the methods of analysis in this enquiry were elegant, it is difficult to say the same for the basic data. This basic data consisted of comments, by the persons being studied, on series of aphorisms, proverbs, quotations and other like statements. These comments were used to assess four of the twenty or so traits of personality which were the basic categories of the research project as a whole. The four traits in question were Optimism, Pessimism, Passivity and 'Desire for the Unattainable'. Other traits like Aggression, Deliberation, Aloofness and so on were tested by sets of questions. For both the comments, and the answers to questions, the subjects of the investigation were asked to 'state their emotional reaction', from plus 2, strong agreement, through mild agreement, zero, minus 1, and strong disagreement, minus 2. This kind of enquiry constitutes what has been called 'personology'.

So far as *answering* such questions is concerned (I would not wish to speak so of those who set the questions), this is a game for boneheads. Proverbs and aphorisms do not belong to us as articles for graded agreement or disagreement. They are formulae that can come to hand momentarily to make a point or to ease a difficulty. The sensible man does not see them as articles of faith, but as loose ideas inviting sometimes a casual kind of social endorsement, sometimes a more thoughtful opening out into wider experience. 'The more you want something the less you get it'; 'real friends are hard to find'; 'every cloud has a silver lining'. These were among the items that the subjects were asked to grade on the five-point scale. I know what I should have done: shrugged my shoulders and put a zero every time. From sensible persons, endorsements are not to be had on such easy terms. But the subject who did put zero to most of his questions was eliminated as 'uncooperative'...

It should be noted that questionnaire-investigations into personality owe much to H. A. Murray's seminal work, *Explorations in Personality* (1938). Murray stresses, however, the distinction and indeed contrast between the technicalities of his book and the intentions of the 'untrained person'.[24] Nevertheless, in the second part of Goldman-Eisler's questionnaire, many of the actual questions (as against the proverbs and so on for comment) also strike one as unmanageable save at a semi-automatic level of response. Consider some of the indices provided in respect of *aggression* (doubtless one is well advised to admit to getting, or at least deserving, a top score in this respect). But: 'are you apt to rebuke your friends when you disapprove of their behaviour?'; 'Do you often blame other people when things go wrong?' One must surely comment, is it not to the point to distinguish whether the behaviour seemed grave or trifling? To know what 'rebuke' is supposed to mean? To settle whether things have gone wrong because someone is to blame, or no one is to blame? Another question: 'Do you try to get your own way regardless of opposition?' My own aggressiveness takes this form: when in the democratic majority, I always try to overcome opposition; when in the other case, contrariwise. 'Do you avoid close intimacies with other people?'; 'Are you employing most of your energies in the pursuit of your career?'; 'Do you feel sometimes that people disapprove of you?'; 'Are you slow in deciding on a course of action?'; 'Do you enjoy playing with children?' The first thing to say, surely, is that one has to brace oneself to make the effort to take such things seriously. Then, perhaps the right thing to add is that the answers to such questions depend on whether one is married or not; in employment or retired; driving a car or changing one's job; or again, on whether the children seem to enjoy playing with you; and (a more fundamental point) whether people sometimes really do disapprove of you, or not. Surely there is a case for saying that those ready to brush all that aside, and be free with their minus 2s and plus 2s in answer to such questions, would in most cases simply have no real personality at all.

Consider another example of the same kind of work: the 'Value Profile Questionnaire' employed by Bales in his factor analysis of the 'value-domain' for individuals partaking in group activity.[25] The basic material comprised about 140 assertions which 500 Harvard undergraduates in the research programme were asked to respond to, this time on a dauntingly elaborate seven-point 'strongly agree... strongly disagree' scale. It is perhaps to the point to observe that the very idea of strong agreement or disagreement is itself a certain crudification of consciousness. True, we often speak loosely in this way; but in reality nothing is strongly true or strongly false, and agreements are about truth. We often, and of course with justice, attach strong feelings to our beliefs, and there are those who, at meetings, are fond of saying that they strongly agree or disagree with what has just been said (it is a comfort to recall the fact that their strong agreement or disagreement will end up, just like the ordinary kind, with just one vote). On the other hand, we cannot always say that an assertion is true or not true. Only too often, its truth is doubtful, or its meaning is unclear. Such difficulties arise, spectacularly, with many of the assertions used by Bales.[26] To start simply with their item 1: 'It is the man who stands alone who excites our admiration'. If we can bring ourselves to spell things out, we must say, 'this generalization is too sweeping, sometimes it is true and sometimes false'. Is that not so? Item 3 reads: 'the ultimate and true reality is above the senses; immaterial, spiritual, unchanging and everlasting'. Some will find this a more congenial assertion than the previous one, others the reverse; but in either case, what remains to be said is that it is really five or six distinguishable assertions. Even a devout Christian, in agreeing with such a statement, would say something like, 'Yes but I want to explain, I'm not sure about "unchanging", and the statement needs adding to about the individual human soul' – and so forth. If we enquire into personality along such lines and forget all such complications, we are looking for something superficial and diagrammatic, for something more like the cartoon of a man than the thing itself.

It is perfectly true that individuals interacting in groups may set up comparatively simple patterns which often take the form of multi-dimensional polarities; all the various forms of taking a lead or following a lead would be one aspect of this. No doubt such polarities can be significantly studied and analysed, in some sense, by the methods that Bales was using. The question is of the level at which this is done. Consider the 'twelve categories' of Bales's system for, in his own words, 'classifying interaction'. Category five is entitled 'gives opinion', and category six, 'gives information'.[27] These are in fact what represent the whole of the more cognitive side of the individual's participation in group activity according to Bales's classification. Yet 'gives opinion' and 'gives information' are, to a high degree, portmanteau terms. Those who 'give information' in a group discussion include those who offer generalizations from their experience; those who provide factual details which constitute evidence for the assertions of others, or alternatively which cannot be explained on the basis of those assertions; those who draw attention to what may be inferred logically from what others say; those who point out logical inconsistencies in the arguments of others; those who claim that a discussion is being conducted in unacceptably reductive terms; and much besides. We all know that such distinctions relate sharply to individual personality and individual consciousness as those terms are understood in everyday use. Furthermore, once such distinctions as those are called to mind, the whole polarity between 'gives information' and 'gives opinion' itself seems crude and confusing of the issue.

In 1958, Inkeles, Hanfmann and Beier conducted an enquiry into 'Modal personality and adjustment to the Soviet socio-political system'.[28] 'Modal personality' means something like one of the representative kinds of personality in a given group. A large number of former Soviet citizens, who were displaced during the Second World War and its aftermath, and who then decided not to return to the USSR, co-operated willingly with this research programme, and were studied in depth. The investigators were not satisfied with, as they expressed it themselves, 'a simple and direct translation of particular test scores into personality traits'. They supplemented tests of the kinds I have been discussing already with what they called 'qualitative material'; and in the end they produced a series of vivid qualitative sketches of what turned out – in plain man's language – to be 'typical Russians' of the kinds represented by the original sample. They 'hoped to arrive at a rich and meaningful picture', and this they achieved. The article in which they published their results makes convincing and human reading.

So, one is dealing in this case with an enquiry where a substantial effort was made to avoid the usual limitations. Yet for all that, one disquieting feature is noticeable all the time; and that is, how inter-personal and other-regarding are the perspectives of the account of 'typical Russians' within this large group. We learn that the members of the group were, in respect of 'modes of impulse control' (an important category in this kind of study), disposed to act out their impulses, subject to a desire for guidance and control from *outside*. They were preoccupied with how far to trust *others*; they cared strongly about loyalty to *friends*. This is contrasted with an American control group: it showed more concern for *impersonalized and public* standards of control: the contrast is interesting because the two contrasted extremes are both equally inter-personal and other-regarding. Again, we learn that these Russian subjects wanted *those in authority* to be fully and firmly directive, but warm and caring at the same time. They were not particularly exigent about definition of rights or regularity of procedure in the *conduct of business*. They showed, in general, a keen awareness of *others*. They freely expressed their criticisms of *others*.

Observations of these sorts made up the staple of the enquiry's findings; and it is easy to see to what an extent they project the individual personality into an external, social dimension. This enquiry, however – I repeat that it seems to have been a more sensitive one than many others – certainly had some things to say about what one would call the inner life of the subjects: for example, that they often displayed fear or despair, or that an optimism/ pessimism polarity was widespread among them. Yet even here, what is striking is how everything is modulated into a social dimension. What gets to be noted down is not that an emotion was felt, that it was part of a subject's inner life; but that it was 'shown'.[29] The evidence about the matter is the subject's response to tests set up by *others*; or the statements that he or she makes about *others*; or it is observation of his behaviour towards *others*. These indices of personality come in the end to seem as if they were what constitutes personality; it is forgotten that they are also indices of consciousness, and that personality without regard to consciousness may be an interesting construct for the social scientist, but is a grave reduction of what we ordinarily mean by the word. Once again, inner re-forms itself as outer. Personality is inter-personalized. In this case as in the other cases, the final outcome seems to be that by imperceptible gradations we are brought to see the individual personality as an aggregate of more or less independent qualities; qualities that in each individual case result in this or that 'profile' for the whole, but seem as if their being collocated as they are was a more or less random process.

If we stop to think, we know that this is not how we regard people and their personalities. We think of them as having a focus and a centre, all their qualities relate to that centre in some sort of organic order. This is what makes them normal and stable adult persons, and not problems for the psychiatrist. In 'real life', as one might put it, we know that sometimes it is difficult to pass from outer to inner; but we think of doing so as the heart of the problem of knowing others, and the philosophers' theoretical difficulties mean nothing to us.

Tolstoy, in his *Childhood, Boyhood and Youth*, was also concerned to portray personality traits among a group of Russians; and he too knew how, in formulating our con-

ceptions of personality and consciousness in others, we have
to rely on outward signs and behaviour, and that that
reliance is sometimes difficult. But his sharp eye for such
signs went with a luminous awareness of their essential
transitivity inward, their status as authoritative expressions
and revelations of inner life. I think particularly of scenes
between the young Tolstoy himself and his brother Volodya.
Sometimes, indeed, those outward signs of inward consciousness are too luminous, too revelatory:

what tormented me most was that it sometimes seemed to me that
Volodya understood what was going on inside me but tried to hide
this...

or again:

who has not noticed those mysterious unspoken relations which
manifest themselves in a barely perceptible smile, a gesture or a
look, between people who live together...? How many unuttered
desires, thoughts and fears or being misunderstood are expressed
in one casual glance, when eyes meet shyly and hesitantly!
  But perhaps my inordinate sensitiveness and tendency to
analyse deceived me in this case. It may be that Volodya did not
feel at all as I did. (*Boyhood*, Chapter v)

In this work Tolstoy is presenting the interplay between
inner and outer as the very nerve of life when it is lived at
the level of full consciousness. 'Since I saw' he writes
elsewhere, 'that Karl Ivanych was in that emotional state
of mind in which he uttered his inmost thoughts, regardless
of his hearers, I sat down quietly...' (*Boyhood*, Chapter viii).
When the worthy German schoolmaster Ivanych is replaced
by a stylish French tutor, the young Tolstoy gets into
difficulties with him, and in the end is convulsed and
tortured with hate and self-hate. At one point his grand-
mother orders him to beg the tutor's pardon. He cannot
bring himself to do it. '"Nikky" said Grandmama, probably
noticing the inward agony I was suffering, "Nikky" she
repeated in a voice more tender than commanding, "can this
be you?"' Later his father also passes dramatically from
outward signs in his son's behaviour, to inward life: beginning at condemnation and anger, and moving through

a kind of hostile puzzlement ('"What's the matter?" he said, slightly pushing me away'), to a quite opposite response: ('"What's it all about, little one?" he asked sympathetically as he bent over me.' *Boyhood*, Chapter XVI). Rapidly, the father is re-ascribing his son's complex behaviour to hitherto quite unglimpsed dimensions of his inner life. Tolstoy writes all the time as one who is aware that, insofar as he fails to reach from outward signs, through to that inner consciousness, he fails of his purpose and omits the core of his subject.[30]

A scene in the first part of the book, when the children of the Tolstoy family go to eavesdrop on Grisha, the one-eyed 'holy man', at his night-time prayers in the attic, sets before us what is at issue. The children are filled with inquisitiveness. They want to see the penitential chains that they know Grisha wears under his shirt. As he prayed, they could hear those chains, that 'knocked on the floor with a dry, harsh sound'. Then Tolstoy writes:

Instead of the amusement and laughter I had expected when we entered the garret, I was trembling and my heart beat...the impression he made on me and the feeling he evoked will never fade from my memory...O Grisha! Your faith was so strong that you felt the nearness of god!

The children slip away in a mixture of childish awe and pins and needles. The holy man hears the noise, and in his devout innocence, makes the sign of the cross towards each corner of the room. In their hurry and disquiet, the children just realize that he does it to drive away the demons he thinks he hears (*Childhood*, Chapter XII).

The scene is all intuition and emotion supervening upon the patterns of idle childish mischief; but it is magical and haunting just because of how easily, how smoothly, Tolstoy moves in it from the shallows to the half-glimpsed depths of the psyche, depths that he makes clear and open to us as much over the thoughtless children as over the elderly half-saint, half-fool. The point of origin, certainly, is the interaction of a group, and a simple everyday one; but what takes its origin from that is a kind of awareness, of all-comprehension, vibrant, nervous, self-transmuting, and rich with growth and consciousness and inner wealth.

In turning from the special field of the personologists, to Tolstoy, we have followed the general course of this book. The chapters which follow are all three about works of literature; and I shall argue that these works do not simply (like the material examined in the earlier chapters) display, to a greater or lesser degree, a changed sense of the individual consciousness, but record that change and reflect upon it. Briefly, what I shall suggest is that Thomas Hardy did something to challenge and reject the 'Apollonian consciousness', and to settle, albeit sadly, for something else; that Gary Snyder recognized and resisted such a change; and that the authors whose work I consider in the final chapter also saw and recorded that change, though they did so dramatically not discursively, and that in effect they made myths for our time out of it.

VI   THE PASSING OF 'LARGENESS'

THE comprehensive, all-comprehending mind, serene and lucid – the Apollonian consciousness: what happened to this idea between, let us say, Shelley's ode 'To a Skylark' of 1820 (where it is conspicuous) and Hardy's poem of seventy years later entitled 'Shelley's Skylark'? For Shelley, the skylark that he listens to in Tuscany is an emblem of the inspired poetic mind. He imagines the bird's 'full heart', full with the spontaneous music of a profuse inspiration. He sees the bird as if 'hidden in the light of thought', with a consciousness of the hopes and fears of the world which is more comprehensive than what others have, and a power to think 'things more true and deep' than mortal men. Even so, however, even if the achievement of the song is beyond them, all men would listen to it and heed it if they could. Shelley thinks of the creative individual, that is, as did Wordsworth: a being of 'more comprehensive soul' than others, but one who is nevertheless bound to others by a deep bond, so that his individual insights will speak to them and for them all.

Hardy is courteous enough to his predecessor, to speak without reserve of Shelley's own 'ecstatic *heights* in thought'; but even at this point, one can see a significant change from the 'true and deep' thoughts that Shelley himself claimed for the poet. Moreover, those laudatory words come only at the very end of Hardy's poem, and seem almost like a polite afterthought. The weight of 'Shelley's Skylark' is taken up with the totally different idea that Hardy has about the bird itself, the singer. It 'lived its meek life', it 'only lived like another bird'. Now, even its dust cannot be found. The obscurity of its life and of its death are total and equal; and what interests the poet, what he thinks deserves to be celebrated, is precisely this limitedness and obscurity.

87

Perhaps one may glance at two other bird-poems by Hardy, both from the turn of the century. 'The Bullfinches' displays a response to what showed itself in 'Shelley's Skylark'. Hardy imagines the bullfinches to sing, not because they are 'hidden in the light of thought', but simply through their own ignorance. Let us sing, one of them says, because we do not know whether today will be our last day. Nor, if it comes to that (this bullfinch seems to have a certain wisdom that the poem has to obscure) does our Mother, Nature, know either. She 'falls a-drowse' at her work of making and running the cosmos, and

> How her hussif'ry succeeds
> She *unknows* or she unheeds.

The other poem is 'The Darkling Thrush'. Here Hardy indeed celebrates a bird's singing in something like Shelleyan terms, writing of its 'ecstatic sound', of how he hears its 'joy illimited' as the missel-thrush sings from a tree-top, under a grey winter sky. But for Hardy in 1900, joy and ecstasy had a very different counterpart *in thought* from what they had had for Shelley. All he is willing to say is that he himself 'could think' that his missel-thrush was responding to '*some* blessed hope' of which the poet himself is ignorant. In the first of these two poems the birds have no foreknowledge, in the second the bird perhaps glimpses something of the future, but the poet cannot discern what it is.

Shelley's poem might be taken as a sign of one major trend in how the nineteenth century was to see both the artist himself, and also (to think for a moment of the novel) the interesting character depicted by the artist. In either case, the point at issue was what Wordsworth had referred to: something like 'comprehensiveness of soul' and amplitude of consciousness. Over and over, the major nineteenth-century writers, whether poets, novelists or thinkers, care about these qualities and seek to display them in their work or to trace them in their subjects. 'Not deep the poet sees, but wide', writes Matthew Arnold, adjusting the Wordsworthian conception but clearly not disagreeing with it; and offering us, in passing, a reminder of the great Dutch panoramists in the field of painting. The novelists sought either to present characters who had such qualities, or to depict the processes whereby, as they grow up or mature, characters come to have them in the end.

Such, for example, are the terms in which Matthew Arnold praised Tolstoy.[31] What shows, he says, in the great works of Russian fiction, is 'a consciousness most quick and acute for what the man's self is experiencing, and also for what others in contact with him are thinking and feeling'. Russian authors are 'absorbed in seeing' – the words are remarkably apposite to the trend of this present discussion as a whole – what the true and full facts of consciousness are like, the 'secrets of human nature – both...external and internal'. 'Great sensitiveness, subtlety and finesse' address themselves 'with entire disinterestedness and simplicity to the representation of human life.' The hints one can find here as to what Arnold was taking for granted about the potentialities of consciousness, and so of fiction, are by now familiar to us: consciousness in 'thought and feeling' is something subtle and capacious, it has its 'secrets', and in pursuing those secrets the writer's own subtle and capacious consciousness will be absorbed, and will open itself to its fullest and amplest, in 'letting his perceptions have perfectly free play'. Later in his discussion, Arnold records one outstanding example, as he sees it, of what such consciousness in the author will generate in regard to consciousness in a character. This comes when he speaks of Anna Karenina: 'The impression of her *large*, fresh, rich, generous, delightful nature never leaves us.'

We are familiar, or perhaps one ought rather to say, still familiar, with the concept of 'largeness of mind'. Cardinal Newman drew upon it in his account of the ideal university:

An assemblage of learned men, zealous for their own sciences...are brought...to adjust together the claims and relations of their respective acts of investigation...Thus is created a pure and clear atmosphere of thought, which the student breathes though in his own case he only pursues a few sciences out of the multitude...He apprehends the great outlines of knowledge, the principles on which it rests, the scale of its parts, its lights and its shades, its

great points and its little...A habit of mind is formed which lasts
through life, of which the attributes are, freedom, equitableness,
calmness, moderation and wisdom.[32]

Apollonian qualities indeed.

It may not be at once clear that Newman and Arnold were
starting, in both cases, from the same fundamental
conceptions about human potentiality. But that becomes
clearer as Newman proceeds; because he finds himself
repeatedly relying upon one form or another of the very
word that came first to Arnold's mind when he was seeking
to identify the thing that made Anna Karenina what she
was. 'The cultivation of the intellect is an end distinct and
sufficient in itself...so far as words go it is an *enlargement*.'
'Knowledge...is an indispensable condition of *expansion* of
mind', Newman also says; though he is quick to add that
that is not enough. If our experience is suddenly, dramatically
extended, he argues, our knowledge may by no means at
once be increased; rather, we may feel, in our confusion,
that we have less than before. But something more fundamental will have changed. We shall have 'a consciousness
of mental *enlargement*'; and the word 'enlargement' then
comes to be the nerve of his whole argument. 'The study
of history is said to *enlarge* and enlighten the mind'; 'the
enlargement consists...in the mind's energetic and simul-
taneous action upon and towards and among...new ideas';
'that only is true *enlargement* of mind which is the power
of viewing many things at once as one whole'.

Such conceptions of what human consciousness could be
like, and at the same time of what it ought to be like, were
widespread in Newman's time. One may find another, very
similar example, in George Eliot's *The Mill on the Floss*,
written some ten years or so after Newman's discussion
reviewed just now. In Book IV, chapter III of that novel,
George Eliot depicts the heroine, Maggie Tulliver, at that
point in life when she begins to grow from a child into an
adult. She goes over the various aspects of Maggie's life, and
then she says that Maggie 'wanted some key that would
enable her to understand them'. That is just what Newman

had in mind when he spoke of 'the power of viewing many things at once as one whole'.

As she reads such books as she can find, and as she begins to think for herself, Maggie begins to make progress. George Eliot writes, 'It flashed through her like the suddenly apprehended solution of a problem...for the first time she saw the possibility of *shifting the position from which she looked.*' Those words are remarkably like what Newman had said about the at first confusing impact of new experience: 'he has made a certain progress...he *does not stand where he did,* he has a new centre'. Maggie begins to 'meditate'; and 'after all her meditations', as the author herself puts it, 'that new inward life of hers' so fills out her whole consciousness that it begins to reveal itself in her outward appearance. Then, for this, George Eliot turns out to use exactly the word Arnold was later to use of Anna Karenina: 'Maggie used to look up from her work and find her mother's eyes fixed upon her; they were watching and waiting for the *large* young glance.'

Hardy's characters also 'meditate'; but if one considers Hardy alongside the cases I have been examining, one finds something different. Chapter xviii of *Far From the Madding Crowd* is entitled 'Boldwood in Meditation'. We find Boldwood in a 'meditative walk' up and down the stables at his farm. In the next chapter he 'went meditating down the slopes with his eyes on his boots'. In Chapter iv of the same novel, 'Gabriel meditated, and so deeply that he brought small furrows into his forehead by sheer force of reverie.' In Chapter xxxiii there are Bathsheba's 'perturbed meditations', and in Chapter xliii the 'contemplations' that she indulged in; and in Chapter xxv, Sergeant Troy's 'virtuous phases of cool meditation'. Hardy however is far from seeing the meditations of these, the four major characters in his novel, as bringing enlargement of vision or mind, and new inward life.

Troy's 'meditative moments' are 'oftener heard of than seen' (Chapter xxv). Bathsheba's 'utmost thoughts' were never distinctly worded by herself, but if they had been, they would have amounted only to a feeling that her instincts were pleasanter guides to conduct than her discretion. Gabriel Oak's thoughtfulness amounts only to 'contemplating a crack in the stone floor', and 'his mental rehearsal and the reality had no common grounds'. Boldwood's response to Bathsheba is in essence one of a meditation which is a profound *in*comprehension. 'He looked at her... blankly.' Whether women were comprehensible and predictable or not, 'he had not deemed it his duty to consider'.

In all these cases, one may almost conclude that what Hardy says in Chapter xxv about memory – 'it may with great plausibility be argued that [it] is less an endowment than a *disease*' – is not far from what he thinks about human potentiality in general for contemplation. Arnold, in 'The Scholar Gipsy', wrote of how 'this strange disease of modern life' (by which he meant, of course, modern life itself) could 'numb the elastic powers'. Today, we have rather lost the ability to use the word 'elastic' of the mind and sensibility. That meaning is one which the nineteenth century seems both to have developed, and to have allowed to begin to pass away. Hardy makes clear that Troy's most deeply felt acts, like putting the flowers on Fanny Robin's grave, spring from inelasticity of mind on the one hand, and blindness on the other.

Yet what seems to be operative in Hardy's mind is not that blindness is bad. Rather that, simply and generally, it is characteristic of mankind. Troy's blindness makes him a little absurd; but Fanny has a blindness that operates quite differently. She

by some mysterious artifice had grasped the paradoxical truth that blindness may operate more vigorously than prescience, and the short-sighted effect more than the far-seeing; that limitation, and not comprehensiveness, is needed for striking a blow.

If Fanny in Chapter xi had 'contemplated' the truth about her distance from the workhouse, instead of determinedly pretending that it was less than it was, she would indeed have found that contemplation, like memory, was a 'disease', because she would have never got there.

In *The Return of the Native*, Hardy's verdict is a similar one.

Clym Yeobright's good looks, when he comes back from abroad, present the onlooker with an intermingling of two things: 'beauty' and 'its parasite thought'. At the close of the passage (Book Second, Chapter VI), Hardy writes much as he did in *Far From the Madding Crowd*. Clym 'already showed that thought is a *disease* of flesh, and indirectly bore evidence that ideal physical beauty is incompatible with emotional development and a full recognition of the coil of things. Mental luminousness must be fed with the oil of life'. Luminousness, comprehension, meditation, contemplation – Hardy indeed had at his call the vocabulary in which the nineteenth century celebrated the powers and range of human consciousness. What he did, though, was to invert their use.

Clym, in fact, gets everything in his life wrong and muddled, precisely through being thoughtful: every reader of the novel will see that that is so. The same is true of Angel Clare in *Tess of the D'Urbervilles*. Repeatedly, Hardy uses the word 'thoughtful' or its like about Clare; but he does so in a kind of sorrowful condemnation. 'He is a pa'son's son, and too much taken up with his own thoughts to notice girls' (Chapter XVII) may not mean much; but that conception of Clare returns. He showed 'a long regard of fixed, abstracted eyes'; 'for the first time of late years he could read as his *musings* inclined him'. 'For several days after Tess's arrival Clare, sitting abstractedly reading...hardly noticed that she was present' (Chapter XVIII). Later in the novel, Angel reflects on how Tess had borne a child to Alec in the past:

Meanwhile Clare was meditating, verily. His thoughts had been unsuspended [that is, he had not stopped thinking about the matter], he was becoming *ill with thinking*; eaten out with thinking, withered by thinking; scourged out of all his former pulsating flexuous domesticity. (Chapter XXXVI)

Two ideas which have come to the fore earlier on are very clear in those words. The first is that 'thought is a disease of the flesh', and the second, that enlargement of consciousness – to be 'deep in thought' – is not the mode in which the flexuous, 'elastic' powers of man develop themselves, because it is the very thing which destroys that elasticity.

Elsewhere one may again see how near Hardy is to the prevailing conceptions of the nineteenth century, although his final position is far away from them. In *Jude the Obscure*, Hardy does something to depict life in Newman's 'pure and clear atmosphere of thought', with a consciousness of 'the great outlines of knowledge' and an enlightenment that is an enlargement of mind – the life of a university. This comes in Mr Tetuphenay's letter to the young Jude: 'I venture to think that you will have a much better chance of success in life by remaining in your own sphere.' The Master of Biblioll College was far from Newman's conception. It could not be said of him that Jude's letter had been an experience such as Newman visualized as the effect of foreign travel or of a visit to a great capital city. There is nothing in Mr Tetuphenay's letter to indicate:

a sensation which perhaps he never had before...He will perhaps be borne forward...He has made a certain progress, and he has a consciousness of mental enlargement; he does not stand where he did, he has a new centre, and a range of thoughts to which he was before a stranger.

His 'terribly sensible advice' to Jude is the opposite of all that. But on Jude himself, its effect is rather what Newman described. Jude reads the letter and it is a blow to him. Then, however, he goes out into the city of Christminster, to the crossroads at its centre, and here, having 'fallen into thought' about the antiquity and also the representativeness of life that this heart of the city shows him (a city not much unlike Newman's 'great metropolis'), Jude does indeed acquire a 'new centre' in a quite precise sense:

He began to see that the town life was a book of humanity infinitely more palpitating, varied, and compendious than the gown life. These struggling men and women before him were the reality of Christminster.

Jude has been 'borne forward' to 'a range of thoughts to which he was before a stranger'; and the close of the chapter is his chalking up, on the wall of Biblioll College, 'I have understanding as well as you.' Yet in the end, this turn of events exactly confirms what has been argued up to now in respect of Hardy. The words that Jude writes on the wall are from the Book of Job, the Man of Sorrows, and everyone knows how falling into thought and having understanding were the very things that brought Jude to disaster.

There appears to be one great exception to all that has been said so far about Hardy. The argument has been, that what Hardy offers his readers with regard to the characters in his fiction, stands in strong contrast to what George Eliot offers, or what Arnold praised in Tolstoy, or what Newman praised as high cultivation of mind. Hardy does not offer to interest the reader in the characters because these have largeness and depth of consciousness; but because, on the contrary, they show the reader how such ideas are grandiose illusions about what humans can achieve; or, if they are not illusions simply, then they are a kind of debilitating and destructive hypertrophy of humanity. There is one great exception, however, and the exception is Hardy himself. Almost throughout his fiction, Hardy preserves one of the basic conventions of what is often called the classic age of fiction. Whatever limitations, of whatever kind, the author depicts in his characters, his own understanding of them and their lives and situations, and his power to shape and govern those things, are without limitation. In such fiction, one might say, the author functions as an individual consciousness that is raised to the level of a natural force – or perhaps a supernatural one. He controls his characters' doings, he comprehends their minds, the judgements he passes upon them have decisive authenticity. His own 'soul' is the 'comprehensive soul' that Wordsworth spoke of. Such is the status that Hardy implicitly assumes for himself. There is no suggestion that, for him as author, consciousness is limited and thought ultimately a disease of the flesh.

Hardy's verse, however, presents him as author in another light. I have argued this at some length elsewhere, and suggested that Hardy's words in one poem – 'No answerer I...' express a prominent theme in his poems and a main aspect of his poetic originality. Hardy was the first English poet to present the author of the poem, not simply the protagonist in it, as an anti-hero. His characteristic stance as a poet may be seen, for example, if one compares two poems in *Late Lyrics and Earlier*: 'An Autumn Rain-Scene' and 'An Experience'. In the first of these, the poet depicts a number of individual figures trudging on to their destinations on a rainy day. One is off to a merry-making, one in a hurry for medicine for someone who is ill, one an aimless vagrant, one a herdsman driving home his cattle. But all, in their absorption and preoccupation, have no place in their consciousness for the rain that falls on them. Last of all is one who (the poem hints) is dead and underground. His unconsciousness of the falling rain is total. In fact, it is this final case that Hardy uses, ingeniously, to suggest to the reader that all the others in the poem are unconscious and unaware likewise. But Hardy himself, as the author, is another matter: he is unaware of nothing. Not only has he a full and even deep awareness of the life of each of the people in his poem, his consciousness is large enough for the attentive reader to see him as thinking about the poem's strategy and how it will mediate its ideas to the reader. This is the Hardy of the fiction.

'An Experience', though, is a poem of another kind. Like 'An Autumn Rain-Scene' in some ways it is a simple poem. Simply, there is something which happens, something momentous, the 'experience' of the poem. Its momentousness cannot be pinned down into fixities and definites, but it brought an aura, a new 'afflation', as Hardy puts it. Yet then, at just this point, the poem begins to modulate the stance taken up by the author. It shows him as delightedly bewildered rather than comprehending. He is astounded, he 'scarcely witted what / Might pend'. His mind was 'cobwebbed, crazed', as it received the joyful something that the poem has as its happy though uncomprehended message. This is no large and luminous consciousness, but something alive yet formless, joyously responsive yet almost blank, and the poem has to issue from this very blankness.

In 'He Follows Himself', the poet is, as he pointedly says

himself, 'in two minds'. Part of him is going (in imagination, we think to begin with) on a journey to the house of a dead friend. The other part of him knows that the friend is dead and desires not to go; but the first part of him reveals at this point that it too knows, and desires to make the journey all the same. Then, at the end of the poem, we realize – or we may just realize – that the 'house' is a grave. The phrasing of the final stanza adroitly jumbles together being in a divided mind over visiting the 'house', and at the same time being in a divided mind over striving to leave it. This is a poignant and haunting poem, but precisely because it so well evokes the confused, amorphous consciousness of the writer. One needs to add, no doubt, that as the strategy and dexterity of the poem come to be recognized, one cannot continue to believe in the confusion of the writer's mind. Quite the contrary. But it is that impression of confusion and amorphousness of mind which the poem seeks to depict as the persona of the writer in the first place.

'The Dream is – Which?' is ingeniously entitled. Though published later, this is one of the pieces from the 1912–13 period when Hardy was reliving his years with his first wife:

> I am laughing by the brook with her,
> Splashed in its tumbled stir;
> And then it is a blankness looms...

'A blankness looms'; the gay vision disintegrates; it is replaced by one that is drab and lonely. That is the repeated modulation of each of the three stanzas. In the second, the lovers sit joyfully together:

> Till a harsh change comes edging in
> As no such scene were there...

Each time, a moment of vivid consciousness dissolves and is negated. True, the closing lines speak of how the poet:

> ...wandered through a mounded green
> To find her, I knew where.

But it is a dreary and minimal knowledge, only drably different from the minimal and dreary state of mind that closes each stanza of the poem.

Hardy records the poem 'Best Times' as 'rewritten from an old draft', and it must be another of the poems recalling his life with Emma. The pattern of it is much the same as that of 'The Dream is – Which?' Each stanza opens by recalling some happy event from the past; but the stress now is upon how that happiness was enjoyed in slight and idle fashion, was cocooned in casualness and unawareness. 'And I did not know...'; 'And I did not think...'; 'And I full forgot...'; 'No thought soever...struck me.' The richer consciousness begins to form, but almost at once it dissolves; or more exactly, not even that: the poem depicts moments of life which were vivid, but lacked fullness and awareness even from the start. Immediately following 'Best Times' in Hardy's own text is 'The Casual Acquaintance', and this poem expresses even in its title how it embodies an experience from which anything like a fuller consciousness is lacking:

> Would I had known – more clearly known
> What that man did for me

Hardy writes. What the man did was merely some 'casual jot / Of service' on the road one evening of hard weather.

> But I saw not, and he saw not
> What shining life-tides flowed
> To meward...

from that casual and unregarded jot. That is the constant refrain or implied refrain in Hardy's poetry. 'No Answerer I'; 'I saw not'. In fact, that second phrase goes a step further than the first. For Hardy, recurrently, the experience out of which a poem came was an experience in which incipient awareness dissolves – a blankness looms, a curtain falls, something comes edging in, the mind becomes cobwebbed, casual, not seeing. A glimpse of Apollonian awareness disintegrates into smaller and sadder consciousness, unseeing not merely unknowing.

One may think, alongside Hardy, of two poets contemporary with his younger years who did indeed seek to represent in their verse the larger, Apollonian consciousness which I have been pursuing. Those two poets were Hopkins, and Meredith. Certain of Hopkins's late sonnets of course speak with great emphasis of the human consciousness at its largest and deepest:

> No worst, there is none. Pitched past pitch of grief,
> More pangs will, schooled at forepangs, wilder wring.

That is indeed far from an Apollonian state of mind, but it is a grief the opposite in kind to Hardy's; Hardy's was 'worst' because it was powerless to so much as grasp the scale of its own predicament. At the same time, Hopkins's grief is not a matter of intensity without scale and largeness. His imagery makes this clear:

> O the mind, mind has mountains; cliffs of fall
> Frightful, sheer, no-man-fathomed...

It is the range and scope of the experience that in large part make it terrible.

Nevertheless, Hopkins's findings about his experience and state of mind remain remote from Newman's in two decisive respects. First, the scale and scope of the experience are sources only of unmitigated, unparalleled despair. Second, insofar as that is not altogether true, it is because those ultimate mountainous pitches and falls of consciousness are – mercifully – brief:

> Nor does long our *small*
> Durance deal with that steep or deep. Here! creep,
> Wretch, under a comfort serves in a whirlwind: all
> Life death does end and each day dies with sleep.

The movement of thought in that whole sonnet bears, in the end, a not inconsiderable likeness to the movement of thought which proved to be so recurrent in Hardy. The larger consciousness is unquestionably there for a while, but it soon dissolves. Much the same comes elsewhere in Hopkins's last poems. The sonnet which begins, 'To seem the stranger lies my lot' is an example:

> Only what word
> Wisest my heart breeds dark heaven's baffling ban

Bars or hell's spell thwarts. This to hoard unheard.
Heard unheeded, leaves me a lonely began.

Once again, the upshot of insight and awareness is sorrowful dissolution into bafflement and emptiness.

One may write, more briefly still, of Meredith; but there is no doubt that in his verse, attempts to register the power of consciousness to expand creatively, and of meditation to be fruitful, are recurrent. One even finds in Meredith that the key word in Arnold, Newman and George Eliot turns up once again:

You a *larger* self shall find

writes Meredith of one who truly responds to 'The Woods of Westermain'. Or one may quote from his poem 'Meditation Under Stars': physically, the poem says, one may be intimidated by the sight of the starry heavens; but man's rational part 'leaps alight' –

To feel it *large* of the great life they hold

and there is the same word over again. The words 'to feel it large' presumably mean 'to feel itself at large in', and the concealed metaphor is therefore one of the open sea, which emphatically underlines the idea of a capaciousness of individual consciousness. But in Meredith's case, all this and much more is worse than useless, it merely compounds the felony. This poet's phrase-mongering and pontificating bravado leave only a total tabloid vacuity, a universe of hectoring catch-phrase. Largeness takes on an inter-stellar emptiness, as if once for all its time were up.

To conclude this discussion, let us return to Hardy for a moment. In his work we are seeing something which begins to look like more than an idiosyncrasy. Are we the witnesses of what T. S. Eliot, in another context, referred to as a 'change that came over the mind of Europe'? If so, largeness and depth of consciousness were ceasing to be a central ambition, it may be because it was ceasing to be a reality that some men genuinely had access to from time to time, or was ceasing to be a genuine possibility for men. Here Hardy's solution for Elizabeth Jane, at the end of *The Mayor of Casterbridge*, is to the point. Certainly Hardy himself thought that what he gave to Elizabeth Jane was the nearest that one could get to the ideal of largeness, and that wanting more than it, was being like the Fisherman's Wife in the folk tale, who in the end wanted to rule over the sun and moon, and so lost everything that she had. What Hardy gave to Elizabeth Jane, as modest but final reward, was 'the cunning *enlargement* [there is the key word again, but its sense has changed] by a species of microscopic treatment, of. . . minute forms of satisfaction'. I believe that those words show how Hardy was representative of a great shift in how, over the past hundred years or so, our ideals and perhaps also our realities have changed.

VII THE POETRY OF THE WILDERNESS

G ARY S NYDER ' S WORK has a special kind of
interest for the present discussion. Various 'nodal ideas', as
one might put it, have emerged in that discussion so far, but
the two of most relevance at this point are, first, the idea
of a narrowing or limiting – or indeed something like
coarsening – of the individual consciousness or of how it is
conceived by those who concern themselves with it; and
second, the idea of a lesser degree of involvement with the
whole panoramic landscape (natural or social) of external
reality. These ideas were prominent in the first two chapters,
and the former of them has of course run throughout, so
far. Snyder is not only convinced that both of those ideas
are valid about our present state of culture; but believes (and
this with regard especially to the natural environment) that
they go together. Failing to be delicately attuned to our
natural environment is both cause and effect of the limited
and coarsened consciousness of modern urban life.

Such a writer, however, is likely to prove to be in a difficult
position. He will be trying to work counter to the tendencies
that he himself believes are dominant in his time. If he is
right, and those tendencies are powerful, even though
inconspicuous, they are likely to affect his work contrary to
his wishes and even, it may be, without his knowledge. What
is powerful, pervasive and inconspicuous is difficult to guard
against, and infiltrates insidiously.

Snyder bases his fundamental condemnation of modern
affluent-industrial society upon the thinking of, among
others, Eugene Odum.[33] Odum, and Snyder with him, see
contemporary civilization as not complex and sophisticated,
but on the contrary, crude and reductive, like a short-term
predatory monoculture where everything depends upon one

single crop or one single energy resource. The single crop upon which modern society depends, while it can, would be a gigantic fossil-fuel harvest. In such an unreflecting and predatory society, the individual consciousness is likely to be narrowed and reductive. Doubtless this train of thought is familiar, and everyone feels something, at least, of its persuasiveness.

Archaic or tribal societies on the other hand are not, as the pundits used to take for granted, simple and primitive. It is they which are like the more mature and developed ecological systems. They are based upon the complex inter-locking of a whole manifold of resources and activities; and because of that they are, like climax vegetation, capable of achieving stability over millennia. They release, promote, and enhance individuality, they do not impoverish it. 'What we call the primitive is a mature system', Snyder writes, 'with deep capacities for stability and protection.'[34] In societies of such a kind, personal consciousness will have reached a level to which our world is largely inimical: 'Society [in the modern industrial world, he now means] providing buffers and protection of an increasingly compli-cated order, so that as it became larger...it protected individuals from...demands for *speed, skill, knowledge, and intelligence*...The personal direct contact with the natural world required of hunters and gatherers – men and women both – a *tremendous continual awareness.*'[35] Or again, 'The Australian aborigines live in a world of ongoing recurrence – comradeship with a landscape and continual exchange of being and form and position; every person, animals, forces, all are related.'[36] I shall return to the matter of Australian aborigines.

This distinction between advanced and primitive society is present everywhere in Snyder's thinking. 'Comes a time when a poet must choose', he says, 'either to step deep in the stream of his people, history, tradition...philosophy... Or, to step beyond the bound on to the way out...possible utter transcendence, possible enlightened return.'[37] Choose, we might say, between being Alexander Pope, or William Blake. But in a primitive society the choice seems to be less

rigid, less disablingly exclusive. 'Primitive cultures...have
...this knowledge of connection and responsibility, which
amounts to a spiritual ascesis for the whole community.
Monks..."leaving the world"...are trying...to achieve
what whole primitive communities...live by daily; and with
more wholeness.' This is where the wilderness has its quite
special place in Snyder's view of things. He writes:
'"Beyond", there lies, inwardly, the unconscious. Outwardly,
the equivalent of the unconscious is the wilderness.'[38] The
wilderness offers to a poet an external reality which will
positively and actively guide him, away from the reductive-
ness of modernity, and into the full depth and delicacy which
consciousness can achieve, and which 'primitive'
consciousness did achieve: Snyder's 'connection' and
'responsibility' as known to the early hunters. Further than
that, and moreover without discontinuity, without necessity
for choice and rejection, the wilderness will guide him to the
unconscious also.

Snyder's poetry is at its best – its most free, spontaneous
and rich – when it registers that going beyond; which is into
an experience of wilderness such as no British poet, so far
as I can see, can have on his home ground today. Here are
American Indians hunting:

> All beaded with dew
> > dawn grass runway
> Open-eyed rabbits hang
> > dangle, loose feet in tall grass
> From alder snares –
> The spider is building a morning-web
> From the snared rabbit's ear to the snare.[39]

In a consciousness of this order there is nothing inane,
nothing to condone, nothing of 'the more you want something the less you get it' and the like. The poet's consciousness
is sharp, searching, pinpoint-fine. The morning dew, the
hunted rabbit, the patiently assiduous hunting spider, all
enter with equal freedom and equal exactitude. The presentation can afford to be curt, because it has seized on essentials
that survey and mark crisply out, that as it were triangulate,

the complete world of the hunter. Is there a dry jest in the word 'morning-web'? Is it used in a double sense? One does not know. But the level at which the whole experience is rendered is clear. 'Are you employing most of your energies in the pursuit of your career?' is not a question one could have put to rabbit, spider, snare-setter – or poet. They are all established and alive in another world from such pontifications.

Here are the opening lines of 'By Frazier Creek Falls', in the collection *Turtle Island*, published in 1974:

> Standing up on lifted, folded rock
> looking out and down –
>
> The creek falls to a far valley –
> hills beyond that
> facing, half-forested, dry
>
> – clear sky
> strong wind in the
> stiff glittering needle clusters
> of the pine – their brown
> round trunk bodies
> straight, still;
> rustling trembling limbs and twigs
>
> listen.
>
> This living flowing land
> is all there is, forever...

Here, on a large and open scale, is a sharpness of vision as keen as that which took in the dead rabbits on a small scale. It effects a taut, laconic integration of everything in the passage. The clear, wind-swept sky brings about the parched, 'half-forested' landscape and at the same time the panoramic view of it. The dry pine-needles and their limbs and twigs and cones can speak to the reader ('This living, flowing land...') exactly because they can seem to 'listen' to the long spread and stretch of the wind as it rustles through them. They rustle, because that wind rustles them. When he writes like this, Snyder's praise of the archaic hunter and his 'speed, skill, knowledge and intelligence', his 'tremendous continual awareness', reflect back upon the writer. At such moments he seems to have just such qualities himself; veritably to be the poet as archaic hunter. Such an opening-out and richness of consciousness is valuable to us all, is a permanently valid pointer, operating against standing weak-nesses, standing reductionisms, in our own lives.

Why does Snyder sometimes fall short of this level of success? What is it that sometimes obstructs his way, and prevents him from achieving, in full measure, what we should expect him to seek, and should predict for him if for anyone? What may it be that prevents him from registering the chosen scene with the delicate yet profound vision that we know he admires and know he often enough expresses? The essay entitled 'Re-Inhabitation' opens with a brief account of an 'elderly Salish Indian' who used to come to the house when Snyder was a boy. This elderly Indian used to sell smoked salmon. The parents are dismissive about the old man – 'He's an Indian' – but their small son recognized the inadequacy and superficiality of their understanding of the pasture- and forest-land they lived in and worked on; and recognized that the travelling Indian knew about these things in another and better way. 'I sensed what he represented, what he knew...He knew, better than anyone I had ever met...', the place itself, the land, and its vegetation, where Snyder lived.

'Then, suddenly, he never came back.' And that is all. It would be absurd to raise objection to this. No explanation is required of why little is said about someone who is only a memory from boyhood; however much he may have embodied Snyder's ideal of a man filled with deep perceptive consciousness of his environment and the life it contained. However: two of Snyder's poems – I have chosen these two out of many that one might have chosen – make this food for thought. The first is section Nine of 'Logging' in 'Myths and Texts'.[40] In fifteen very short lines the poet tells of how he worked on the mountainside all day one Friday, and then hitch-hiked off to see a girl. He had to hitch-hike two hundred miles. When he reached the place they both had a bath and made love 'night-long'. Then 'all Sunday' they 'softly talked', and after that Snyder hitch-hiked back to work.

This poem does not seem to have the same terseness and brevity as that about the rabbits and the spider. Nor can we see it as a decorously reticent poem, which would not be Snyder's way and might not satisfy us either. Rather – though I hardly know how to put this – it seems like the work of a man undergoing some influence which impels him on, away past what otherwise he might prefer to dwell on. 'August on Sourdough. A Visit from Dick Brewer' is curiously similar, not simply in its subject, also a brief visit, but in how that subject is treated:[41]

> You hitched a thousand miles
>   north from San Francisco
> Hiked up the mountainside   a mile in the air
> The little cabin – one room –
>   walled in glass
> Meadows and snowfields, hundreds of peaks.
> We lay in our sleeping bags
>   talking half the night;
> Wind in the guy-cables   summer mountain rain.
> Next morning I went with you
>   as far as the cliffs,
> Loaned you my poncho – the rain across the shale –
> You down the snowfield
>   flapping in the wind
> Waving a last good-bye   half hidden in the clouds
> To go on hitching
>   clear to   New York;
> Me back to my mountain   and far, far, west.

Self-evidently, one can detect here the same quality of apprehension as what showed in the hunting passage, or that about Frazier Creek. We pick up the quality of vision that shows in the 'glass meadows and snowfields' of the big windows in the look-out cabin; in the taut, pointed suggestiveness of 'rain across the shale'; and in the contribution of a detail like the visitor going into the cloud, but downhill. The idea of the 'glass...snowfields', which can stand almost realistically by itself, endows the 'glass meadows' with a meaning more than what they get from just the 'big windows': perhaps they have also the unreal quality of this remote mountain-top world. Yet, once again, there is an almost total reticence, even a kind of a telescoping and blurring, about the actual meeting that took place between the two consciousnesses; until this poem, along with the other, begins to bring to mind how Snyder's poems quite often record meetings and conversations; but meetings presented, with surprising regularity, in a manner abrupt and almost dismissive:

> ...talked to the guy, he says
> If you see McCool on the other tailcrew over there
> Tell him Moorehead says to go to hell.
>
> ('Bubbs Creek Haircut')[42]

or elsewhere:

> I picked up an Italian tree-surgeon
> in Port Angeles once, he had all his
> saw and tools all screwed and bolted on
> a beat up bike.[43]

Those last words are something said to Snyder by a man he has hitched a lift from: it is one brief, snatched, random encounter boxed, as it were, inside another. Along with these, there is the fragment of conversation with the man who shared a barn-loft with a girl 'back in 1910';[44] or the brief account of the friend in the Northern Sierra whose car hit a doe, and they found a perfectly-formed embryo fawn in the doe's womb;[45] or lines like:

> Stopped in the night
> Ate hot pancakes in a bright room
> Drank coffee, read the paper
> In a strange town, drove on...[46]

or:

> On our way to
>   Khajuraho
> the bus stoppt, we ate
>   guavas

cheap...
    in the square
dusty village somewhere on the way.
                    ('On Our Way to Khajuraho')[47]

It is not unreasonable to begin to find something strange, when a writer so often portrays human contacts in such terms as these in his poetry, although in prose he will say, 'the community is essential to the creative act; the solitary poet figure...will become less important. I prefer to be with my friends – which is the creative context.' The point is not in the least that the poems that Snyder writes about being with his friends are bad poems. First, they are not that, and second, if they were that would still not be quite the point. The point is that they are poems of a kind significantly different from the kind we should particularly expect him, of all people, to seek to write and to be able to write about friends, and that we should value if he did write. There is an entry in the 'Japan First Time Round' diary: 'an ant is dragging a near-dead fly through the moss-woods by the tongue'.[48] It is a superb observation. It epitomizes much of what is impressive in Snyder's work. But I find that it returns to the mind also, as a kind of disquieting reminder, a disquieting reminder of what in his creative work he so regularly omits – he of all people, one gloomily reflects.

Snyder is not the only American writer to see good in the life of the woodman. Here is a passage from Thoreau's *Walden*:

who should come to my lodge this morning but a truly Homeric man...a Canadian, a wood-chopper, and post-maker, who can hole fifty posts in a day, who made his last supper on a woodchuck which his dog caught.   ('Visitors')

This Homeric man had learnt, from a priest, to read Homer aloud in Greek, but not to be able to translate. The passage goes on:

a stout but sluggish body, yet gracefully carried, with a thick sunburnt neck, dark bushy hair, and dull, sleepy blue eyes, which were occasionally lit up with expression...He was a great eater of meat, usually carrying his dinner to work...cold meat, often cold woodchuck, and coffee in a stone bottle...sometimes he offered me a drink...Frequently he would leave his dinner in the bushes, when his dog had caught a woodchuck by the way, and go back a mile and a half to dress it...after deliberating first for half-an-hour whether he could not sink it in the pond safely till nightfall...He interested me because he was so quiet and solitary, and so happy withal...as he sat on a log to eat his dinner, the chickadees would sometimes come round and alight on his arm and peck at the potato in his fingers.

This same man would often write the name of his Canadian parish in the snow, in an elegant handwriting, and with the correct French accents. He must be the wood-chopper, Canadian by birth, who turns up elsewhere in the book, and who took a French newspaper, 'to keep himself in practice'.

Thoreau's leisurely pace, occasionally slow-moving wit, bookish style, and limited admiration for the Indian (he probably knew only Indian societies that by his time had been gravely disrupted) may make today's reader tire of him; but he is reminiscent of Snyder in a number of ways. He has a similar care for nature and the wilderness (insofar as he knew it) and he too depreciates town life, 'progress', and modernity. He believes as Snyder does in the Muse; he is drawn to Buddhism, which he prefers to Christianity ('God is in the letter *Ku*, as well as the letter *Khu*', he quotes); and he even writes a paragraph, in the 'Tuesday' section of *A Week on the Concord*, which expresses almost the same dedicated and 'sacral' view of the hunting activity as Snyder's. Yet there is something about that woodman which bears a curiously half-confirmatory, half-contradictory relation to Snyder. To a substantial extent (not, true enough, entirely) Thoreau's woodman has the sensitive oneness with his environment, the 'tremendous continual awareness', that Snyder admires. Further than that, he is totally lacking in the urban and predatory acquisitiveness that Snyder detests. Yet, he is such a character as Snyder almost never even begins to depict.

Thoreau depicted him without hurry, as if that was right for the task he took in hand. He dwelt with affection on him: relaxed yet sensitive, 'withdrawn' yet communicative. In writing like that, Thoreau showed that he knew what it had been, traditionally, to depict a man, a character, in the round. People act and speak, they think and have opinions, they have an appearance subject to subtle, continuous variation. From all this the observer, given time, patience and concern, builds up a sense – spacious, multitudinous yet meticulous – of their inner life and the wealth of their consciousness. In the chapter in *Walden* on 'Reading', Thoreau reveals that he knows about the literary tradition of such characterization, speaking of – to name no others – not only Shakespeare, but also Aeschylus and Homer.

Recurrently, Thoreau writes out of certain assumptions, familiar to us though perhaps no longer fashionable among us, about what there is to depict in men (and so, what is a pressing call and claim upon the writer) and what are the ways to depict it. Often, his best characters have a good deal of what Thoreau sees as coming from a life of labour in more or less wild conditions, and of nearness to a natural environment. He records in *A Week on the Concord* (the 'Tuesday' section) how once he had tramped up into the wilds of Connecticut. There he 'found...a few wild and hospitable inhabitants', and in the end he sought a night's lodging of a farmer at the head of a remote valley in the mountains. This farmer is a gruff, seemingly rude man. He takes each of Thoreau's attempts at conversation the wrong way. Yet, seemingly so unapproachable, he is quick with pride and love for his remote corner of the world, and 'as he lighted the lamp I detected a gleam of true hospitality and ancient civility, a beam of pure and even gentle humanity, from his bleared and moist eyes'. Besides him, there is the aged, Wordsworthian man Thoreau meets on the road, who also responds roughly at first, but then suddenly takes off his hat, and prays God to take care of the stranger. Then there is the young stone-mason 'repairing the locks in a solitary part of the river', who listened to Thoreau's account of himself, and then asked more questions, 'but temperately still, and always turning to his work again', and who helped him through the locks 'with a sort of quiet enthusiasm' ('Tuesday'). There is the 'soldier lad' that they meet deep in the woods, 'going to muster in his full regimentals', who starts by 'holding the middle of the road', but loses his nerve ('Thursday'). All Thoreau's people have a kind of rounded humanity, a gentleness that goes with humility in them before the 'where' and the place of life. Thoreau can lay claim to such qualities himself, as writer, because he depicts them with such unhurry and such affectionate care. He, as well as his people, manifest what Snyder admires.

There are perhaps two reasons, of different kinds, why Snyder does the same thing less often or less well. The first would be that he seems to have two radical interests, or convictions, which in their final tendency somewhat diverge. On the one hand there is his respect for human potential ('Man is a beautiful animal. We know this because other animals admire us and love us'[49]), and his respect for the truly, fully human and humane. But on the other hand, Snyder seems sometimes to wish to write of Nature, wild things and the wilderness, and to drop the human part of the natural spectrum out of the picture altogether, or at least put it last. 'We're just starting, in the last ten years here, to begin to make songs that will speak for plants, mountains, animals and children.'[50] In the *Crater Mountain Lookout's Journal* of 1952 is a note reflecting on the situation 'If one wished to write poetry of nature...'; but almost the next words are: 'reject the human'.[51] The poet immediately qualifies this by considering 'the tension of human events... against a non-human background' as something that there is anyhow a likelihood one need not reject. Even so, at this point the element of tension, of divergency, in his thought is inescapable.

One of Snyder's poems, 'A Walk',[52] underlines this point if we compare it with, say, Thomas Hardy's poem 'A Wet Night'. Both of these pieces are about the poet himself, taking a walk in a wild place. Snyder's trek up to a lake high in the mountains enables him to give effect to the best qualities of his verse: its nervous variations of rhythm, its close, sharp observation, its lean absence of padding. But in content it seems almost like an effort on the poet's part to be rid of the human dimension: to create an environment that comprises wilderness, and poet, together but together in isolation. 'Murphy fishing', is how Snyder's piece about this Sunday morning walk begins. The poet soon says goodbye to that isolated human touch. He climbs away up the 'rock throat', among the 'deer tracks', 'boulders big as houses', and hen quail fussing over her stone-coloured chicks. By the high lake, the only sign of humanity is an old, rusty, derelict cookstove, relic of men who have long disappeared from the lonely scene. The poet seems almost to brush it aside. As he comes across it, his only comment is, 'stoppt and swam and ate my lunch'.

Again, there is nothing necessarily to fault in such a poem. Simply, it is one kind of poem and not another. Thomas Hardy's 'A Wet Night' helps to bring out what kind, because in some ways it is similar, and in other ways it is so clearly a contrast. To consider it at some length is worth while, because the discussion is concerned with Snyder's verse as part of a wider subject: the ways in which the arts, considered generally in our time, sustain or do not sustain our whole sense of full and integrated human personality and potential. Hardy's poem has its own substantial interest from this point of view.

A WET NIGHT

I pace along, the rain-shafts riddling me,
Mile after mile out by the moorland way,
And up the hill, and through the ewe-leaze gray
Into the lane, and round the corner tree;

Where, as my clothing clams me, mire-bestarred,
And the enfeebled light dies out of day,
Leaving the liquid shades to reign, I say,
'This is a hardship to be calendared!'

Yet sires of mine now perished and forgot,
When worse beset, ere roads were shapen here,
And night and storm were foes indeed to fear,
Times numberless have trudged across this spot
In sturdy muteness on their strenuous lot.
And taking all such toils as trifles mere.

This poem contrasts in two ways with Snyder's. First, it dramatizes not simply a state of consciousness, but a transformation of consciousness on the part of the poet. His first thought, of the personal and self-enclosed hardship he underwent, is dispelled by a larger-minded and more humane thought. In the second place, there is something distinctive that enables this transformation to occur. It is, that the poem also dramatizes (though briefly no doubt) the consciousness and actions of many of the poet's fellow humans over a long tradition of the past. 'A Wet Night' is by no means one of Hardy's most important poems. Its interest, in the present context, is how clearly it belongs to an important tradition of poetry: the tradition where poems are among the helps to us in conserving a sense of human consciousness and of its fullness and goodness and power.

I suggested that one reason why Snyder's poetry does less than we might expect in giving us such a sense, was that there seems to be a certain degree of mixed motive in his work: part of him rather wants to turn aside altogether from the human, even at its best. Perhaps there is another reason also why his poetry does less than one might expect to implement and express his convictions about human consciousness and potentiality. This relates less to the content of his verse than to what, frequently, is its mode of organization. Here are two examples:

> crystal towers   gleam for a hundred miles
> poison oak hedges, walled child garden
> and the ring mountains holding a cool
> basin of pure evening fog
> strained thru the bridge
> gold and orange
> beams of cars wiser than drivers
> stream across promenades, causeways
> incensed exhaust.
>
> ('Hymn to the Goddess San Francisco
> in Paradise', 2)[53]

> Catch fire, move on.
> eurasia tundra reindeer herds
> sewn-hide clothing, mammoth-rib-framework tent.

Bison, bear   skinned and split;
  opening animal chests and bellies, skulls
  bodies just like ours –
pictures in caves.
  Send sound off the mouth and lips

formal complex grammars transect
  inner structures & the daily world –

big herds dwindle...
ice age warms up
learn more plants, netting, trapping,
bow and arrow.   dogs.[54]

What sort of organization do we encounter as we look at
these passages?

I mentioned it in the first chapter of this book, when I
spoke of *The Waste Land* and of how certain parts of that
poem could be transposed without changing the sense or the
success of the work. What we are concerned with is what
Pound called the 'mode of superposition', which has so
much been the staple and the characteristic feature of
Modernist verse. In the passage about evolution, there is a
number of more or less separate, discrete items. To some
extent they are strung out along a time-scale, but by no
means entirely so. The items in fact fall into a series of
sub-classes, and those sub-classes have a loose chronological
sequence; but within each sub-class the relation is one of
simple co-existence, and this co-existence is mirrored,
grammatically, by paratactic juxtaposition. The reindeer
herds, the tundra, the tents out of mammoth rib, the
clothing of hide – or again, the bear and the bison, the
cave-pictures, the beginning of language – or again, the
traps, nets, boats, dogs, bows and arrows, are set side by side,
without conjunctions or temporalizing prepositions. The
poem does not offer any temporal sequentiality, as among
each group of items. Even the boundaries between the
sub-classes (for example, the three groups of items that have
just been distinguished) are left in part open, so that it is
uncertain whether the temporal relation between the successive sub-classes is succession, or overlapping, or whether no

temporal relation whatever is indicated between two successive sub-classes. Again, there is nothing whatever necessarily wrong with such a mode of organization. All this is simply characteristic of 'mode-of-superposition' poetry.

The San Francisco passage introduced a complication. It used a kind of semantic embedding-process which is more or less impossible in standard prose, though familiar to us in verse of most periods, if perhaps most conspicuous in the verse of our own period. Consider a brief passage like:

> ...pure evening fog
> strained through the bridge
> gold and orange
> beams of cars wiser than drivers
> stream across promenades...

Even that brief passage juxtaposes – 'superposes' – considerably more statements than is obvious. I read in it at least the following:

the evening is pure

the evening fog [by contrast] is impure

the evening fog is pure

the evening fog is pure because it is strained [i.e., filtered] through the bridge

the evening fog strained [i.e., struggled] through the bridge

the fog is strained [i.e., filtered] gold and orange

the beams of cars are gold and orange

the cars are wiser than the drivers

and perhaps also:

pedestrians are wiser than drivers.

For it to be possible to unpack such verse, and be left with an array of superposited items denser and more numerous and more intricately inter-related than we at first expected, does not affect the fundamental question; and the fundamental question is whether the mode of superposition in general, whatever its exact form, tends to present, and so to entrench, human consciousness as one kind of thing, rather at the expense of its being another kind. Pound said that Browning was his poetic father, but a Browning stripped of superfluous words. He developed this idea in the context of such attitudes as we find in 'Hugh Selwyn Mauberley' – a curt, dry resolve not to 'maintain "the sublime" / In the old sense'; not to joint the 'liars in public places'; not to be one with the Mr Nixon of the poem 'In the cream gilded cabin of his steam yacht' counselling Mauberley to '. . . give up verse, my boy / There's nothing in it'.

So, on the whole, superposition came in as a way to achieve the terse, business-like style of the note-taker, rather than the pontificator's rhetorical *longueurs*. Earlier, indeed (as in W. E. Henley's taut, note-like poems 'At the Hospital'), something similar had been developed to express mental states that more traditional poetic means could not easily represent: consciousness between waking and sleeping, or weakness and illness. McLuhan pointed out long ago that the delirium sections of Tennyson's *Maud* were composed in a twentieth-century, Poundian style. Perhaps this is a mode of expression into which the mind naturally falls when it is so taxed that it grinds to a halt ('On Margate Sands / I can connect / Nothing with nothing'), or when it is too full to reduce its thought to order ('These fragments I have shored against my ruin'). The mode of superposition, with its density, absence of verbiage, lack of connectives and (as I mentioned earlier about *The Waste Land*) partial randomness, enabled the poets of the earlier part of this century to do all these things.

But there was a price to pay for these new powers and resources. Writer and reader, both of them, are inconspicuously led away from commerce with the kind of individuality which involves consciousness at its most large, self-conscious and luminous: consciousness manifold, abundant and receding (like those Dutch panoramas) into the depths of its own order, consciousness 'lost in thought', and as such, pregnant exactly with Snyder's 'deep capacities for stability and protection', his 'tremendous continual awareness', his 'speed, skill, knowledge and intelligence'. Rather, superposition has a silent momentum of its own, and easily modulates into the avowedly unintegrated, the laconic and dry, even the sceptical, cool, casual. Doubtless this is a tendency only, and doubtless it may be overcome. When the conditions he chooses are most favourable to him, or the difficulties in his path are at a minimum, Snyder indeed overcomes it. Some of his best poems are the result. But here it is the innate tendency itself, and the cases of only limited or partial success, that are most to the point. Snyder's case is especially instructive. It offers to tell us a good deal about the tendencies relating recent developments in the arts and perhaps also in general, to the presentation of consciousness and to the preservation of a full and deep sense of what human individuality may be.

Snyder's reference to Australian aborigines was to the point for the present discussion. It is interesting to compare, in as general terms as possible, some of Snyder's poetry with some of the poems that have come from those aborigines: because theirs is the poetry, of all that we know or ever shall know, I suppose, that is most completely from wilderness territory, and by people who formed for themselves exactly the kind of primitive culture of which Snyder has spoken. I mean, a mode of life that left their wilderness territory completely and permanently intact: a genuinely successful 'climax vegetation', culturally speaking, that achieved perennial validity in an almost uniquely hostile environment. It may be that the Australian aborigines created that way of life because the arid lands of Australia simply could not be made into arable by any early farming methods; and also, because the native fauna, very largely marsupial, simply did not provide a basis for herding, or indeed for any domestication of animals whatever.

A hundred years ago, it was widely believed that the aboriginal population did not have any true language at all, only a gibberish. The first work known to me that effectively records any aboriginal poetry is A. W. Howitt's *Native Tribes of South-East Australia*, published in 1901. Probably one has to accept the translations in that book with reserve, but if we may attach any weight to them, we have already a handful of lyrics which reveal a clear sense of human intimacy, dramatic situation or even humour and delicacy of feeling. Brief as these texts are, I do not see how one can miss those qualities in them:

> Why did you cut your beard off, long ago, young man?
> There is the girl, she is girl asleep, in her mother's hut.

or again:

> Roll up the twine, girl over there, the little twine,
> Little sweetheart; I shall go to the hollow and wait for
> you.[55]

These transient scraps of song point in another direction from Snyder's 'made love night-long' or 'talking half the night'. Their terseness seems to emerge from an awareness that is complex, yet inward and buoyant. Their few quick strokes draw upon our pre-existing comprehension of such situations; and they convey to us, with a certain precision, more than they overtly state. At the same time, this complex inwardness tells us about the aboriginal author, invites us to recognize his sympathy and empathy towards those in his song. Something is reminiscent of Thoreau and the woodland figures whom he wrote of as so close to himself.

These songs are a little like the *Djarada*, or sexual-magic songs, that a modern Australian anthropologist with a fluent professional command of the languages of the tribes he has studied, Ronald M. Berndt, has recorded in great profusion from north-east Arnhem Land in the northern tip of Australia.[56] These are all men's songs, because the women would sing their songs only to Berndt's wife (also a distinguished anthropologist in the same field). Some of these invitation-songs, as Berndt provides them in transliterated form together with word-for-word translations, have again a strikingly terse sense of dramatic situation and of human inwardness and feeling. In the examples which follow I have sometimes minimally expanded the text so as to make it easier to follow out of the context of Berndt's book, but have tried also to retain the terseness, which is what creates and establishes the mastery of a human love-situation:

> the chicken hawks
> kark kark kark

> they cry as they fly
> so many of them together
> kark kark kark
> as they fly
> so many of them together
> as they fly down, as they fly low.[57]

The girl has gone out into the bush, and the man cannot see her, but he knows that she is there. Moreover, he knows just where she is, because he can see the hawks dropping down low over her head. So, he sings the song for her to hear. When she hears it she in her turn knows that he is there; and she feels the magical influence of the song enter into her. Here is another *Djarada* song of the same kind:

> the rain and the hail
> run down over her;
> the hands of the rain;
> over and over
> and spread out wet on the ground;
> the hawk's cry
> kark kark kark!
> a girl – what a girl.[58]

The next example is a woman's song, recorded by Catherine Berndt from the Bathurst and Melville Islands. A widow is singing to her dead husband, but also singing replies for him, putting words into his mouth. We might begin by saying that she sings for him what she thinks he might sing if he could. Then it occurs to us that perhaps it would be truer to say that she gives him the words that, in spite of all, she wants to hear from him; and the poignancy and depth of how personality and consciousness are evoked in the song become unmistakable. One has to imagine, as the song proceeds, what are the wife's words and what the husband's:

> Why do you come every day to my grave?
> Because your posts are painted and ready:
> Come on, get up from that grave...
> I saw you dancing just now,
> Shaking yourself as you danced:

Why not come to me here?
I'm not old, I'm too young...
Well, I'm waiting for you here;
I'm glad my wife's coming near me;
You'll be thirsty, I can't give you water;
I'm taking you to a dry, waterless country.[59]

In the two songs for men, one might even say that the
more cosmological contours of this body of poetry begin
unobtrusively to show. The chicken hawks do not appear by
chance alone. In some way they become the man's allies
(and perhaps the girl's too). He 'sends the cry to get her',
Berndt records from an aboriginal informant. Similarly, the
rain or hail is more than just itself. It stands for various liquid
things that will flow, from man or woman, when the work
of the magic has reached its climax. These songs develop
their human situations and the life of consciousness within
them, as deeply intertwined with the totality of life and
process throughout the wilderness environment. They
emerge from a primary conception neither of 'reject the
human' nor of 'accept the human'; but one in which such
limiting and programmatic conceptions have never arisen.

More interesting, though more difficult to discuss briefly,
are the major sacred song-cycles, which used to last over
many days or even weeks, and which constituted the great
religious festivals of the northern tribes. These were based
upon the same fundamental linkages between the human
and the environmental, but in a reverse direction. The long,
communal songs dramatized the lives of primal, supernatural
beings who first peopled the aboriginal lands, and did so
through the teeming outcome of their own sexual intercourse
during the initial pilgrimage–exploration journeys. The
people of later times thought of these ancestors as literally
the authors of the festal songs. Thus the festivals, in both
their musical and their sexual dimensions, were nothing but
re-enactments of the life-histories of the original divine
ancestor–authors.

Those festivals were timed for the great natural turning-
points of the year, like the coming of the monsoon. The
nubile women were one with the great cumulus-clouds of

the rains as they blew in from the ocean, and the sexual or generative fluids that occur in the celebration were the rain and the lightning that were to restore and – it was thought – forever preserve the environment. So, the great mythical characters of the cycles were developed, and could be developed, in the song-cycles, because there was a natural environment, in profound association with which it was their essential nature to develop.

That is the picture which emerges from the work of Ronald and Catherine Berndt about the extreme northern tribes, those dwelling in Arnhem Land. T. G. H. Strehlow, in his remarkable work, *Songs of Central Australia* (1971), writes of the Aranda tribes of the central desert. Strehlow was the son of a German missionary at Hermannsburg in Central Australia, and had the extraordinary advantage of being trilingual in English, German and Aranda. A man of wide reading in English and European literature, he could consider the Aranda songs in a context which included not only Shakespeare, but Icelandic Saga, Beowulf, the Hilde-brandslied, and Dante. He records how the Aranda sacred song-cycles involved a belief that every human being had two souls. One was a personal soul, which was annihilated at death; the other was immortal, was the re-incarnation of one of the totemic ancestors, and would be re-incarnated many times again. It was the mother alone who decided which was the ancestor re-incarnated in her child; and she did so in a remarkable way which casts a beam of light upon the profound unity, in the aboriginal cosmology, between the human consciousness, and the environmental reality, which is Snyder's ideal. She it was who, at a certain moment in her pregnancy, would feel this second, divine soul enter the unborn child. How was this determined? Here was the remarkable thing. It depended entirely upon where she happened to be at the time. Every locality without exception (one must remember that the Aranda landscape is excep-tionally desert and featureless) would necessarily be where one or other of the tribal ancestors had emerged from the earth (which was eternal, and had never been created), and then actually shaped the topography of the place. On death the ancestor had re-entered the earth at that same spot, so that one aspect of him (or her) remained physically embodied and present in some sacred rock or tree or other feature of the scene. The deep attachment of the aborigine to the homeland was entirely an attachment to this specific place. He himself was the transient, spiritual re-incarnation of the divine being, who at the very same time continued in existence, in the landscape, in some localized material form. There, surely, was the *ne plus ultra* of Wordsworth's sense (as he records it in the prefatory note to *The Excursion*) that the individual mind is 'exquisitely fitted' to the natural world, and the natural world to the individual mind. Upon the basis of such an underlying cosmology and metaphysics of man, the 'poetry of the wilderness' was necessarily, totally and ultimately humanized.

It may seem as if these observations on aboriginal poetry have digressed from the main train of thought. But if it is true that aboriginal poetry exhibits a particularly deep and complete unity between awareness of consciousness in its fullness, and awareness of the natural environment as one with consciousness and fostering consciousness, there has been no digression. That integrated aboriginal response is the sort of response that Snyder above all admired and has sought to achieve. But one cannot say that he achieved it through his efforts as fully and wholly as the aboriginals did through spontaneity. If then we pursue the matter, and ask why not, the answer lies partly in the difficulties such an attempt must encounter, if it is made in our time and from the standpoint of our society. Partly, those difficulties may be from within literary conventions: conventions apt for the poetry of Pound or Eliot are likely to do certain things more readily than they will do what Snyder has wanted them to do. But besides that, and perhaps more important, there is the basic difficulty of a man who wants to do what his time is moving away from: one who seeks a large, delicate, sensitive consciousness in a world where such consciousness is not a dominant ideal, but recessive.

One contemporary Australian painter, Russell Drysdale, has in recent years done many paintings of aboriginals, and these portraits are much to the point here. Virtually none of them are to be seen in public collections in either Europe or America. Drysdale's portraits of aboriginals (as likewise some though by no means all of his sketches of white Australian bush-rangers and the like) strike one as deep studies of consciousness, of sitters 'lost in thought'. How is this achieved? Their heavy bodies, misshapen through age or toil or child-bearing, and often stressed by the big hands that gently grasp the thighs (there is one like this, painted in 1961, called *The Woman Mangula*) or seem just about to descend on the body and touch it, are firmly and unmistakably human. Yet the faces are mysteriously less so. Often this seems to have been achieved by setting the face in deep shadow (*The Young Mourner*, 1960), or by the features being barely hinted at (*The Rainmaker*, 1958; *The Puckamanni*, 1958).⁶⁰ Occasionally, at least to an English eye, this seems to have been achieved simply by the distinctive, unfamiliar cast of aboriginal features in themselves. Then, where the eyes are visible, they often look to be slightly unfocussed; and this, with the almost full-face pose that Drysdale usually adopts, has the effect of making the sitter fix a penetrating, meditative gaze at one and the same time upon the spectator as the spectator looks at the picture; and also, as if lost in endless enigmatical contemplation, upon the distance, the horizon beyond and *behind* the spectator. It is as if the endless, almost featureless, moonlike landscape of the Central Australian wasteland, which so often forms the background to these portraits, stretched away behind us also, as we have the portrait before us; and as if the figure in the portrait is staring, nostalgically and perhaps sometimes in bewilderment, 'lost in thought' over the hereditary topographical panorama. These marvellous paintings stand apart from other mid-twentieth-century art, and recall some of the great portraits and figure studies – utterly different as of course they are – which I considered in Chapter 1.

VIII CONSCIOUSNESS BELEAGUERED

Here is a poem by the Orkney-Islands poet, Edwin Muir:

THE RIDER VICTORY

The rider Victory reins his horse
Midway across the empty bridge
As if head-tall he had met a wall.
Yet there was nothing there at all,
No bodiless barrier, ghostly ridge
To check the charger in his course
So suddenly, you'd think he'd fall.

Suspended, horse and rider stare
Leaping on air and legendary.
In front the waiting kingdom lies,
The bridge and all the roads are free;
But halted in implacable air
Rider and horse with stony eyes
Uprear their motionless statuary.

Muir was a true and integral poetic spirit, and a man who profoundly understood what it was to be an individual consciousness in all its fullness. He believed, however, that such human potentialities were today somehow at risk. His poem 'The Rider Victory' is to the point here, because it seems like a poem about a twentieth-century work of art: a painting by Picasso, or a sculpture by Brancusi or indeed Reg Butler. From the poem, we cannot tell whether Muir wishes us to take that phrase 'motionless statuary' in the last line as literal or metaphorical – whether the poem is about a living man, or a stone figure, or both. If it is about a piece of sculpture, there is a piece called *Horse and Rider* done in the 1950s by the Italian artist Marino Marini, which in its intense and stressful immobility, its melodramatic

self-assertiveness, its appearance of being suddenly, grandi-
osely halted into posturing futility, is remarkably close in
feeling to Muir's poem.

Another and comparatively well-known contemporary
painting, Salvador Dali's *Temptation of Saint Anthony* (1946),
also brings Muir's poem to mind. One of the horses in Dali's
work, in its grotesque and melodramatic posture, recalls
Muir's line, 'Leaping on air and legendary'. I mention these
examples to show how near Muir's irony comes to what we
can find depicted, with such formal interest and such energy
and intensity of emotional response, in certain works of
contemporary visual art. For of course, Muir's poem is irony.
It is full of a restrained but intense consciousness of what
men do to themselves when they make themselves indis-
tinguishable from monumental statuary; when they have,
in Yeats's memorable phrase in his poem 'Easter 1916',
'made a stone of the heart'.

Consciousness of this danger, and of the ultimate contrast
between those who overcome it and those whom it overcomes, was recurrent in Muir's poetry.[61] One well-known
embodiment of that is his poem 'The Combat'. This combat
is fought out endlessly, in some obscure and anonymous
corner of the cosmos, between the 'crested animal in his
pride' – a monstrous heraldic creature, all self-assertion and
violence – and the 'soft round beast as brown as clay',
unarmed and helpless, but made invulnerable by a simple
kind of courage and faith, an integrity of goodness that
cannot conceive of goodness being defeated by evil. This is
the duellist that hopelessly loses every round:

> ...I never saw
> A beast so helpless and so brave

but seems like winning the battle:

> The killing beast that cannot kill
> Swells and swells in his fury till
> You'd almost think it was despair.

Allegories are perhaps always susceptible of more interpreta-
tions than one; but in this case, two things are clear. The

first is that Muir has in mind the contrast between a de-humanized humanity, of violent intensity and simplified, crudified bravura, and a humanity that retains its humanity in full. The second is that in the poem he sees the latter as thrown perilously on the defensive, as having to fight an endless battle such that one can barely see why it is not endless defeat.

That almost-endlessness of human struggle is a conception that recurs in Muir's work. In the poem 'Telemachos Remembers', the poet thinks of the legend about Penelope the wife of Odysseus; and of how, over the many years that Odysseus was away at the Trojan War and thereafter, she outwitted the suitors who plagued her to admit that her husband was dead and to choose a new husband from amongst themselves. What she did was to say that she would choose one, as soon as she had completed the weaving of a ceremonial robe, perhaps a funeral shroud, for her father-in-law, the father of Odysseus. She worked at the garment all day long, and all the suitors could see her doing so. What they did not see, was that every night she unpicked what she had woven in the day. Muir's poem contrasts these 'Figures in the web she wove', with herself and with Telemachos. What the 'half-finished heroes...a horse's head, a trunkless man' did was, they 'came and stood and went away'. But Penelope's 'pride and fidelity and love' went on unchanged, year after year, and thereby saved her from a 'matchless wrong'; and her son, now an adult, at last understands the meaning and the full humanity of what she did.

Another of Muir's poems, entitled 'The Annunciation', describes the moment of time depicted in countless religious paintings – a unique moment of conversational, intimate oneness between the natural woman and the supernatural angel:

> See, they have come together, see,
> While the destroying minutes flow,
> Each reflects the other's face
> Till heaven in hers and earth in his
> Shine steady there...

Momentarily, each of the two beings is utterly filled with the consciousness of the other, remote as in truth it is. Momentarily they are at the same level of being, and the nearest we can come to understanding it or entering into it, is perhaps to see it as a moment of individualized human consciousness raised to its highest possible level and potentiality. This momentary oneness is depicted in many traditional Annunciation paintings (paintings that are, as I mentioned in passing in Chapter 1, portrait-like studies of individual figures, and ambitious landscapes, all in one); but in a certain respect, Muir's poem departs from them all. The Annunciations of the Quattrocento and the Renaissance depict a setting and a background that the painters strove to make worthy of their subject. Architecture is of celestial, golden proportion and spaciousness, landscapes all serenity and beauty. Nature is shown perfected by art, so that it may be worthy of the occasion.

Muir sees the Annunciation differently:

> Outside the window footsteps fall
> Into the ordinary day
> And with the sun along the wall
> Pursue their unreturning way.
> Sound's perpetual roundabout
> Rolls its numbered octaves out
> And hoarsely grinds its battered tune.
>
> But through the endless afternoon
> These neither speak nor movement make,
> But stare into their deepening trance
> As if their gaze would never break.

The 'increasing rapture', the 'great...wonder' of the 'trance' (that word is thrown into prominence by the way in which it is the only unrhyming line-ending in the poem) is a rapture of marvellously enriched consciousness. But that occurs in an environment wholly other than itself: an environment where the norm is the hoarse grind of noise and the ephemeral passing-by of the anonymous and undifferentiated, a footstep and nothing more. It was never Muir's purpose to denigrate ordinary life and ordinary people. Over and over, his poetry expresses respect and love for them, and a deep conviction that men can enrich and humanize their lives until, one might say, every moment becomes annunciatory. What he denigrates and condemns is Victory Riders, heraldic figureheads, crested human animals in their pride. Even so, when he came to depict a moment of complete and perfect human consciousness, spontaneously he saw it as an enclosed world, necessarily set apart. If what was outside could get inside, that enclosed and perfected world would suffer some great reduction. Muir understood the nature of the enriched, 'Apollonian' consciousness, and cared most deeply about it; but he did not see it, in his own time, as in the ascendant.

In fact, one can almost say that in these poems of Muir's, what we find can be regarded as, in one way or another, the creation of smallscale *fables* which embody the real situation that has shown itself in one after another of the preceding chapters. By that I mean what might be referred to as fables of the destroyers of individual humanity ('The Rider Victory', 'The Combat') or on the other hand of the individual refusing to succumb to the enervation of consciousness ('Telemachos Remembers') or enjoying a moment when consciousness, though perhaps isolated, is uniquely full ('The Annunciation').

Muir wrote an autobiography, and gave the first version the interesting title of *The Story and the Fable*. As he used these words, the 'Story' was simply the sequence of events seen straightforwardly in temporal terms: the everyday 'what happened' of his life. Such a story, however, when you contemplated it, fell into a more fundamental pattern: into a kind of ultimate sequence, the story in its essential phases, conceived more or less in generic terms. This is what he meant by the 'Fable'. There is no reason to think that any and every sequence of events will release this deeper rhythm. Many self-evidently do not; and it is an open question, to say the least, whether every human life will do so. Muir wrote an autobiography because, slowly, he came to sense that his own life did indeed reveal such a pattern, one that gave a certain meaning to having been alive.

It may well be that this distinction is illuminating for the study of all forms of narrative, not autobiography or biography alone. It is not the same as that conceived of by the Russian Formalists, sixty years ago, between 'fable' and 'subject'. For them, 'fable' was more or less what Muir meant by 'story' (such, alas, are the intricacies and frustrations of literary study), and 'subject' meant the particular slant and perspective given to that sequence of events, through the devices and methods chosen by the writer and characteristic of his art. Nor is Muir's distinction between 'story' and 'fable' at all like that familiar to us from recent Anglo-Saxon criticism of narrative, especially Shakespearean dramatic narrative: the distinction between 'story' ('o dear yes, the novel tells a story', E. M. Forster whimsically lamented) and 'theme'. Here, 'story' meant either 'fable' or 'subject', it was no great matter which, and 'theme' meant either some moral quality or value conceived in itself, or some general proposition, about value or occasionally about facts, with regard to experience. One disadvantage of this approach was that the critical polarity which was set over against the mere 'what happened' of the work ignored, or even obscured, the temporal dimension, the sequentiality, proper to fiction of whatever kind. As a result, narrative works tended to be assimilated to discursive ethical essays made concrete, or perhaps merely colourful, by flights of imagery. But Muir's conception of 'fable' as the fundamental and generic pattern that contemplation revealed in 'story' is essentially a temporal and sequential conception.

With Muir's distinction between the 'story' and the 'fable' in mind, and with how some of his poems seem like fables or mythical representations of fundamental aspects of our recent culture in mind also, it is to the point to consider three major novels of the past several decades. These three novels are, two of them, English or Welsh, and one, Australian: John Cowper Powys's *Wolf Solent*, published In 1929; Wyndham Lewis's *Self Condemned* (1954); and Patrick White's *The Eye of the Storm* (1973). What I have in mind to do might perhaps be regarded as a form of content analysis, rather than literary criticism in the most obvious sense. For the present purpose I shall assume (what is no great extravagance) that these are all works of substantial or major literary importance. All three are germane to the present discussion in that, in varying ways, all concern themselves with what human consciousness is like when it is at its amplest and most enriched, even its most many-sided and paradoxical; and (to anticipate the conclusions of this chapter) what I think will prove to be true is that these three novels read, to a greater or lesser extent, like fables, in Muir's sense, of the gathering 'Slumber of Apollo' that this book has been pursuing.

For Powys in *Wolf Solent* (as is usual in his major novels) this sense of human consciousness and its paradoxical multi-dimensionality is part of a wider pattern running through his whole sense of experience and reality. Powys has, for example, a distinctly post-nineteenth-century conception of cause. He rejects Meredith's 'army of unalterable law' idea so far as human behaviour is concerned. Wolf Solent goes to the cemetery where his father is buried and (half expecting it) he sees there one of his father's former mistresses. He has vowed that, if he should see her on this particular day, he would make off as fast as he could. Yet instead of that, he pulls off his cloth cap with effusive humility, steps over the 'intervening mounds', and greets her. Or again, we read:

here he was, with only one single, simple, and world-deep craving...to spend his days and nights with that...*mysterious* and mortal *consciousness*...Christie. And yet, for reasons comparatively superficial, comparatively external to his life-current, he was steadily, day by day and month by month, building up barriers between himself and Christie. (p. 288)

Beyond this non-rational or supra-rational sense of cause as it affects humans, and operating more widely still, lies Powys's intuition that even non-human and inanimate reality shares, in some dimly apprehensible way, the depth, strangeness and life of human individuality.

This latter aspect of Powys need not be developed here; and perhaps enough has been said already, to bring out his idea of the largeness of human consciousness. Powys writes of the '*living, conscious human soul,* different in its entire being from his own identity', that Wolf Solent glimpses within the beautifully nubile physical presence of his wife Gerda; or of the 'vast tracts of unknown country...here were two far-extending continents' which is his final thought about the two of them, not physically so much as psychologically, when they fall asleep together; or of the 'irrationality' that he sees dominating both his wife and his mother when they first meet; but it is an irrationality 'drawn from some reservoir of life-energy that was richer, more real, more strange and vibrant than the lumpish bewilderment with which he confronted it' (pp. 156, 291, 386). Such a conception makes itself felt everywhere in this novel, as in Powys's other novels.

Self Condemned and *The Eye of the Storm* are based on other principles. Their authors are satirical rather than poetic novelists, and their interest is largely in the portrayal of characters whose individuality fails of the luminous depths and largenesses that interest Powys. Yet certainly in *Self Condemned* there is one character who stands in contrast to all the others as, at first, an Apollonian character in a full and direct sense. René Harding is a distinguished academic historian whose work has acquired celebrity on both sides of the Atlantic. He is no arid intellectual. He is genuinely attached to his wife, he finds her unfailingly attractive, he is a dutiful and considerate son, loyal to his family and considerate, at least until insulted, to its members. What, though, is central to his personality is to be unfailingly rational and objective; and to exercise the free and considered choices of conduct that those Apollonian qualities permit.

This sets him in contrast to the other characters in the book. In the exercise of those qualities, and in the clearest possible awareness of the temerity and in a conventional sense the probably disastrous unwisdom of the choice, he decides to resign his Professorship in London because his new and disturbing insights into history make it impossible for him to teach the academic conventionalities he is expected to teach. 'Most people', he says, defending his decision, 'think *collectively*, I agree. But they do not usually think very clearly. They have no pretensions to *being individuals*. They are a collective individual, a group of some sort...I had *to isolate myself...and think the matter out* by myself' (pp. 22–3). That resignation is the act that sets the novel in motion and, as the tragedy proceeds, it is what makes René 'Self' condemned. In an act of self-authentication, he resolved to be more than a collective man, his personality a mere arithmetical product of the social life and organization dear to personology.

Elizabeth Hunter, the central character in Patrick White's *The Eye of the Storm*, is in fact herself the 'Eye' of the storm that rages all round her – nurses, solicitors, children, housekeepers – as at the age of eighty-six she engages in her last dazzling performance, her terminal illness. An immensely rich Sydney society-widow, she lives in her luxury villa in the suburbs, and she seems, at first reading of the book, far away indeed from Wolf Solent's preoccupation with his own 'inmost integrity', or René Harding's objectively and rationally formed 'wish to act upon a heroic moral plane'. Rather, she seems a monster of patronizing snobbery, endless and absurd female vanity, and lifelong predatory sexuality so intense and so effective that even at the age of seventy she was able to set a respectable Norwegian professor, an engaged man, retreating back to base in order not to be inveigled by her mature charms (that, anyhow, is one possible reading, though a good deal in the novel is left open-ended, and for the reader to take in more ways than one).

On reflection, there is more to Mrs Hunter than that. She is far from simply a ridiculous, glamorous Struldbrug. In the first place, the earlier stages of the 'what happened' in this book are created for us by White's flash-backs, which occur chiefly in her vivid and capacious if elderly mind. In this respect, she is a larger consciousness than any of the other people in the book. Also, she is a woman of formidable cleverness, of innate. unchallengeable superiority. She simply outclasses everyone she meets. By an unerring sceptical intuition she understands everyone about her, knows exactly what they want and how instead to get what she wants herself. She knows how to forestall all their initiatives without so much as putting her own cards on the table. Through the bizarre perspective of immense age, she presents us with a curious kind of heroic individual consciousness. More than that again: as the past fills out for us, her total image becomes profoundly different from that of the monster of half-senile egotism that we register at first. The fact is, her lifelong innate superiority came from her like a radiation. On the holiday visit that she and her grown-up daughter pay to friends at their seaside house on an island off the coast of Queensland, it was she who could immediately strike the right note, put their hosts at ease, superbly take over the cooking, enchant the children with her flashes of intuition and fairy-tale generosity, and bring out the dry-as-dust Professor. 'Merely by opening her mouth she made others laugh', writes White (p. 368). When the hurricane comes, it is this seventy-year-old woman, left alone and with the house smashed to match-wood, who proves to have an almost magical will to survive, who lives half-drowned in the bunker, and has a moment of ineffaceable, visionary lucidity in 'the eye of the storm'. Her brilliance and success infuriate and baffle her awkward, rigid, conventional-minded daughter; and as for her son, Sir Basil Hunter, the celebrated and by now elderly actor, he knows himself in his heart of hearts for a successful old second-rater who would have been upstaged every time by his genius of a mother.

One further point about Mrs Hunter shows her for a larger consciousness than appears at first. Although she made his life a misery in many ways, there is a passage in the novel which indicates that Elizabeth Hunter had a profound if tangled kind of love for her husband Alfred, and recognized, even through the mists of egotism, his superiority to herself and her inadequacy before him. Alfred has died before the novel begins; but as his presence fills out in this complex book, he becomes the dominant figure of its earlier years. He lacked his wife's brilliance and good looks and panache. His were the more – the word comes too appositely not once again to use it – the more Apollonian virtues of self-restraint, self-effacement, dignity and above all, comprehension. He was a reading man. His widow found with surprise what a library of books, read and re-read, he had collected at the up-country station where his work lay. There, he and his workmen lived with great simplicity and on terms of mutual understanding and respect. His wife never came.

I believe that one can therefore identify a fundamental pattern, a 'fable', in three stages, in this book. In the earliest stage on the temporal scale – the reader has to re-construct this for himself, out of the flash-backs – the central figure is the dignified, rational, reserved figure of the father. The second stage is dominated by the brilliant, charismatic presence of Elizabeth Hunter herself. The third stage comes mor or less with her death, when her children, her lawyer (an erstwhile lover, needless to say), and two of her three private nurses (their names are Sister Badgery and Sister Manhood: the names again speak for themselves, and Sister de Sanctis, the saintly one, has retired from the scene) take over from her. It is an aimless and random world, of shabbily esurient theatre-people, and of contracts, wills, lawyers, jewellers, airline hostesses, job-hunting, package holidays, ridiculous social gossip. The great wealth of a single and exceptional individual has become the pointless, trivial extravagance of a crowd. Beneath (if that is the way to put it) the varied 'story' of this elderly invalid and her personal encounters can be detected a 'fable': and its three phases are, first, the phase of Apollo (the husband); second, that of charisma (the wife); and third, something like what Weber called the institutionalization of charisma, among all the posthumous non-entities at the end of the book. Unravelled from its flash-backs and its intricacy, the story of the book seems to pass through these three generic phases. The first two could be likened to the phases in art, pre-twentieth century and twentieth century respectively, which transpired in Chapter I of this book. To what might the third be likened?

Powys's hero in *Wolf Solent* is not very obviously an Apollonian figure; but in the frequent references in the book to the 'psychic power' of the 'recesses of his nature', to his 'secret life-current' and the like (pp. 172, 288), he undoubtedly represents his creator's concern for the larger, deeper consciousness. Perhaps one ought to concede that he is a fusing of the Apollonian with the Dionysiac or charismatic. We read of the 'intoxicating enlargement of personality that used to come to him from imagining himself a sort of demiurgic force, drawing its power from the heart of Nature itself' (p. 161). Yet unquestionably he is a representative of the thinking, reflecting, self-questioning potentiality of consciousness. The novel starts on its course when, having delivered, in a mood of exasperation with his London schoolroom, a violent diatribe against modern civilization (and in that, he is clearly much like René Harding), he gives up his job and chooses to return to the deeply rural Dorsetshire of his ancestry. Against that archaic yet bustling panorama – it is rendered with all Powys's rich detail and power, and the structural analogy with the situation in Dutch landscape is obvious – against that background, Solent first emancipates himself from the influence of his strong-minded mother (he lived with her while in London); and then establishes himself within a variegated yet integrated traditional society, and marries the simple, physical, in a sense primitive, and beautifully nubile Gerda. At the same time, Solent is attracted to a friend of Gerda's whose name is Christie; and for a while it seems as if he may enjoy both women and, in a certain sense, be the dominant figure in the whole situation of the book.

Christie is unlike Gerda. She is more delicately made, more intellectual, more independent. Her sexuality – it is there all right – is unpredictable, wayward, evasive. She is a little what used to be called 'fey'. Her nature has a unique, radiant poignancy that eludes definition, but that desolates Wolf's heart as he comes to realize that he has let the one chance to possess her slip through his fingers. All the same, Gerda his wife is no country lummock of a girl. One of the best local features of the book is how Powys develops her independent womanliness. Simple she may be, a plain country artisan's daughter, but within those terms she has will, spirit, independence, and above all, radical intuitive self-hood and power. She is vitally herself. All this is well symbolized in her unique gift. The finest of English song-birds is the common blackbird. Gerda can suddenly break into a ravishing, overwhelming imitation of the blackbird's song. Solent is astonished and dumbfounded when first he hears it. In other words, if the elusive Christie is a charismatic figure, Gerda has a charisma of her own.

I omit, needless to say, a great deal of this encyclopaedic novel as it proceeds. But the later stages of the book enigmatically darken, and they confuse and trouble the reader. Suddenly, inexplicably, Gerda loses her marvellous gift. Her marriage becomes tortured and meaningless. 'Life has scotched her, just as it has scotched me', Solent reflects, wretchedly, at one point (p. 530). Solent himself finds that he is more and more trapped in the very social group where he thought to establish an independent and mature life. He becomes a cog in the machine, humiliatingly financed by a *deus ex machina* in the shape of an English lord, a distant relative of his mother, who among all the rest apparently seduces his wife; or at all events does something that abruptly and mysteriously restores her miraculous bird-whistle. The love between Solent and Christie is mutually confessed but remains unfulfilled. Circumstances take her off to a life of meaningless obscurity in the 'backwater' of the nearest large town. Solent realizes that 'his inmost integrity' is shattered. We read that 'he could not shake off the feeling that his soul had become a drifting multiplicity without any nucleus' (p. 621). Surely, on encountering those words, it is impossible not to recall the approach to individuality as in Chapter VII: multiplicity without nucleus.

In other words, if in the first phase of this novel Solent's enlarging, maturing consciousness is central, and in the second phase the two charismatic women, Gerda and Christie, are central, there is then a third, represented by the motto Wolf coins for himself in the closing pages, '*Endure or escape*' (p. 633), or by his closing words: 'Well, I shall have a cup of tea' – that last infirmity of the English mind. In this closing phase, each character in the narrative has his or her allotted social niche – the Weymouth 'backwater', the little

house in the lane, the country school classroom that Wolf
feels himself doomed to for the rest of his days; and all,
though peaceably enough, seem to be left with the limited
consciousness that such a life-style invites or constrains:
'Endure or escape.'

It must be clear by now that the present train of thought,
in respect of all three of these novels, will lead to the
conclusion that their stories are different but their fables are
the same. The fable-pattern in Wyndham Lewis's *Self
Condemned* stands out more lucidly even than the others.
First comes the rational man, the objective mind, the
self-determining chooser, René himself, dominating a society
of amiable puppets like his silly little wife, or the noisy,
teeth-flashing, grinning 'Tyros' (Lewis's own word for this
particular type in his drawings) like his exceedingly disagree-
able brother-in-law. Or, again, there are the sub-human
automatons, violent, hilarious or absurd, like the bibulous
public-school house-master who affronts René at a dinner-
party, or the Harding's Dickensian London charlady. Such
characters continue to surround René and to contrast with
him during the dreadful days in the war-time Canadian
town of Momaco (Lewis and his wife were in fact stranded,
for the war years, in Canada, and the name 'Momaco' may
be a fusion of 'Toronto' and 'Montreal'). Here we meet the
effete but egotistical connoisseur Furber, and Affie the
macabre hotel-housekeeper, gleefully slaughtering the in-
sects with her gas-gun.

As the novel proceeds, however, René becomes less
comprehending and capacious-minded; while his sexy
puppet of a wife changes in a contrary direction. 'I would
do anything you asked me to do, and go wherever you
wished. I did not know that I would do that once. But I know
now' (p. 239). Where, one finds oneself reflecting, lie the
powers of thought and largeness of consciousness now?
White's novel comes back to mind: one of the characters
says, of Mrs Hunter, towards the close of that book, 'In the
end I feel age forced her to realize she had experienced more
than she thought she had at the time.' It is exactly the same
movement of mind as Hester's. In extremity and adversity,

René's wife – 'Essie', she is called – is the one who is transformed and enlarged. Lewis the intellectualist draws upon an unexpected poignancy and power as he develops her nostalgia, that becomes an obsession, for England; and at the same time, depicts the deepening self-effacement of her love for René, as well as the occasional outbursts of resentful but helpless despair that now round out her characterization and culminate in her suicide.

In this last phase of her life she becomes, one may say, a human individual veritably possessed by a single, all-mastering desire or 'mission': to put before René, merely by her existence, her presence, the second-rate-ness of the Canadian academic and social scene (as, of course, we are shown it in the novel), and to lead him home. The fixity and intensity of her desire to do that are boundless: when she sees she will fail, killing herself is all that is left. In other words, in her limited or perhaps muted way, she too is a charismatic character; and her very name, or rather nickname – Essie, *esse*, simple Being – invites the reader to see this; much as he is told, early in the book, that René is 'half-brother to Everyman' (p. 121). René's names are meaningful also. He must have been called 'Harding' because, over the novel as a whole, he indeed hardens, indurates, loses his humanity; and René, because he is an apostate, he reneges – not in resigning his Chair early on in the book, but in the third phase, after the death of Hester, when the novel ends with a 'glacial shell of a man', a man who 'had become an automaton' and in reality was *dead*, establishing and institutionalizing himself in the ultimate institutionalization – we are told – of a major Chair at a great American university.

Here it is to the point to recall what came to mind, towards the close of the first chapter, about the supermarket and the parking-lot and the pleasure-drive. René has got himself into that world of total choice but empty preference. Curiously, that same quasi-world, mock-world, comes with the close of *The Eye of the Storm*. On their two different airliners, two different air-hostesses ask Mrs Hunter's daughter, the Countess de Lascabanes, and the roué old Sir Basil, what they would like. 'Nothing', the Countess replies. She may choose what she likes now, but there is nothing to prefer. Sir Basil opts for a whisky. When it is done, he opts for another, which proves as null as the first. How many of us have done the same?

I mentioned Edwin Muir's 'crested animal in his pride', and the recurrent sense in Muir's poems that the truly humane human consciousness, in all its spacious aliveness, is somehow under siege, is threatened by giant forces less exalted but seemingly more powerful than itself. Wyndham Lewis's hero uses the same mythical language, at one point, to speak of a threat that he in his turn recognizes.

A *dragon* has made its appearance in this century. It is not a reptilian animal about fifty yards long...it is a far bigger animal than that...one may...almost see its fiery being in the minds of men...We are little, powerless, short-lived creatures...it is supernatural, of vast powers, and ageless. We cannot possibly know why, at certain periods, these monstrous things appear among us and then disappear again. Only, it is the best and only advice. *Mind your own business.* (pp. 133–4)

What is the nearest we can come to those words? It is Powys's *Endure or escape.*

So, in the end, one is left with a sense that all three of these novelists, besides the various story-tales that they choose to tell and that doubtless came to a greater or lesser degree out of the detail of their own experience – an old high-society Australian lady dying, a young man going back to his ancestral landscape, an academic and his wife in war-time Canada – had, also, one single fable-tale to tell. This was the tale of how the striving, self-mastering, all-comprehending, Apollonian consciousness is, in our own century anyhow, under threat; as Muir's humanized brown bag of a creature was under threat. They seem all to bring up, from the depths of the mind rather than its surface, the spectacle of a single pattern: a pattern whereby that spacious consciousness will be succeeded by a narrower, but intensified, charismatic and Dionysiac consciousness; and then, how that will in its turn be succeeded by a consciousness reduced and institutionalized: in the end, if you like, a 'personologist's' random, atomized summation of inter-personal checks and balances. At any rate, these three outstanding authors, in what were major works for each one of them, seem to have wanted to rehearse that underlying pattern: what I venture to call something like a single common dread.

If Lewis's dragon, or Muir's crested monster, really have begun to come (or it may be, to come once again) into the life of our century, is it not likely that even the creative artist who stands for what is opposite to it, may find some powerful but insidious current that partly turns his efforts into what plays no part in his intentions? This, I suggested, was what transpired over Gary Snyder. He exalts depth and fineness in human consciousness, but in the event does not so often portray it, at least in others, as you would think he would wish to do, or would achieve. He exalts deep and full human relations, but the relations he depicts are often in skeletal form; they are ephemeral, casual, even brusque. A world of random contact seems to force itself into the world of a gifted man whose most cherished ideal is just the opposite. 'There are a thousand writers who can draw adequate characters till all is blue for one who can tell you something about hell-fire...there just isn't room for normal character drawing.' That is what Malcolm Lowry wrote when his publishers demurred about *Under the Volcano*.[62] The three novels that I have been discussing all register a fabulous transition from exalted humanity to, in one form or another, hell-fire. If I had to produce an illustrated edition of *The Eye of the Storm*, I should think long about de Kooning's hypnotic, ravaging series of *Woman* paintings, done in the 1950s. To illustrate the essential nature of the closing pages of *Self Condemned*, where all character and humanity have departed, few paintings would be more to the point than some of Lewis's own major canvasses: like *The Surrender of Barcelona* (1936), or *The Crowd* (1914–15: also called *The Revolution*). What do these paintings show, or those of de Kooning, but humanity lacerated into hell-fire, or atrophied into automatism?

One is inclined, after reading these three splendid novels, all of them conceived in tragic terms, to envisage the 'fable for our time' that they rehearse as a fable of slow-moving but spectacular disaster – Lowry's 'hell-fire' in one sense or another. If, however, one makes the kind of intellectual effort that respect for the Apollonian consciousness, its detachment and breadth of vision, itself demands, one can see that that response is excessive. To be sure, a certain limiting or narrowing of individual consciousness, of range and depth and fullness of mental life, is a not unreasonable thing to expect to find, over a period like the past century. This has been a time during which increasing population and ubiquitous 'media' (starting merely with the cheap daily newspaper) have largely abolished lonely environments and periods of solitude, and has also been an age of the ubiquitous 'trouble-saver' (like the word *case* for Fowler). More and more, it could be argued, life has become outward and communal, and most of us have become able to live it without much effort of thought, or contemplation and planning, or even much receptivity to environment. Society and machinery do those things for us. So, there is nothing surprising in the thought towards which this discussion has been moving.

Also, it could be said, a still wider survey of various fields of human activity would quite possibly produce more evidence along much the same lines. One such field, for example, might be that of educational theory as between Montessori and Herbart on the one hand, and Dewey towards the end of the last century on the other. All three (and rightly doubtless) were preoccupied with the overt processes of learning and so of teaching; but with the two former this seems to have accompanied a preoccupation with the inner life of the student, with the nature and realities of 'enlightenment' as a series of events of private inner consciousness, as was not so with Dewey. Another field which, much later, shows the tendency is that of literary theory. Recent 'Deconstructionist' criticism may certainly be said to put forward a conception of the author altogether less Apollonian, conscious and all-comprehending than that in general acceptance not long ago; and I have not pursued this matter, only because I have to some extent done so recently elsewhere.

For all that, however, this remains true: should the facts about a broad and major transition in what might be called 'the terms of life' indeed be as this discussion has suggested, that that is a disaster – a 'dragon' – does not necessarily follow. To someone like myself it easily seems that way, because to admire Wordsworth's 'man of more comprehensive soul' who is at the same time, through that very fact, deeply one with his fellows, was a formative idea and ideal in my youth. But the comprehensive soul which is true to itself will tell us that life may be lived along many lines, and that it is wise to be slow to pass judgements, especially adverse ones.

Of course also, many and divers things have been happening over the past hundred years. In regard to human affairs, if ever one thinks that everything points in one and the same direction, the likelihood is that one simply sees everything moving towards where one is somnambulating oneself. Moreover (and I have repeatedly tried to do justice to this), exceptions to the various trends and tendencies suggested here may easily be found. All the same, before we can pass judgement either way, we need to know. What evidence there is, exceptions and all, needs to be assembled, arranged and reviewed; reviewed in fact, unassumingly but thoroughly, by what must be itself an Apollonian kind of awareness. For myself I can say, with Berenson's 'in-eloquent' creations, that I have 'no urgent communication' to make. I have tried to set out what has come to my notice. Then it is the reader who has to exercise what, at the beginning of this book, we saw Nietzsche calling Apollo's 'ordered control' and 'wise serenity', as he considers the varied evidence.

NOTE ON REPRODUCTIONS OF PAINTINGS

SOME readers may find it convenient to have references to easily accessible books in which they will find reproductions of the works of art which I have referred to or discussed. Piero della Francesca's three paintings are all reproduced in Kenneth Clark's *Piero della Francesca* (London, Phaidon, 1951). Rembrandt's *Self-Portrait aged 63*, and *David Harping before Saul* are reproduced by J. E. Muller, *Rembrandt* (London, Thames and Hudson, 1968); his *Margaretha de Geer* is available as a postcard at the National Gallery, London. The Koninck *Entrance to a Forest*, Ruisdael's *Forest Entrance* and Hobbema's *Road into Forest* may all be seen in reproduction in W. Stechow, *Dutch Landscape Painting of the Seventeenth Century* (London, 1966). Photographs of Lipchitz's two sculptures appear in his *My Life in Sculpture* (1972), and there is a splendid photograph of Moore's *King and Queen* sculpture at Shawhead in John Rothenstein's *British Art Since 1900* (London, Phaidon, 1962). The paintings by Malevich which are referred to on page 12 and 18–19 are reproduced in Camilla Gray's *The Russian Experiment in Art, 1863–1922* (London, Thames and Hudson, 1962), and Dubuffet's works appear in the Arts Council Catalogue of 1966 (see note 8), save that the *Woman Chanting* may be found in reproduction in E. Langin, *Fifty Years of Modern Art* (English Translation, London, Thames and Hudson, 1959); which also reproduces Tamayo's *Man Singing*. Picasso's portrait of *Fernande* is reproduced in Christopher Gray's book cited in note 11, and his *Ambroise Vollard* is in H. L. C. Jaffé's *Picasso* (London, Thames and Hudson, 1964) and elsewhere. The paintings by Marinetti, Severini and Russolo may be seen in Marianne W. Martin's *Futurist Art and Theory* of 1968. For the du Maurier and other cartoons mentioned in Chapter II, see notes 17 and 18, and for the works by Russell Drysdale, see Geoffrey Dutton's monograph on Drysdale (London, Thames and Hudson, 1964). Needless to say, reproductions of all of these works of art may also be found elsewhere, sometimes in many different places.

NOTES

1 Clark, *Piero della Francesca* (1951), p. 40.
2 Letter to J. H. Reynolds, 3 May 1818.
3 B. Berenson, *Piero della Francesca, or the Ineloquent in Art* (1954), p. 7; p. 6.
4 '...jene massvolle Begrenzung, jene Freiheit von wilderen Regungen, jene weisheitsvolle Ruhe des Bildnergottes'. *Werke*, ed. G. Stenzel (1967), I, p. 605.
5 J. Lipchitz and H. H. Arnason, *My Life in Sculpture* (1972), p. 50.
6 *Ibid.*, pp. 44–5.
7 *Ibid.*, p. 20.
8 Arts Council Catalogue, Dubuffet Exhibition (1966), p. 6.
9 *Ibid.*, p. 42.
10 *Ibid.*, p. 29.
11 See Christopher Gray, *Cubist Aesthetic Theories* (1968), pp. 117–18.
12 Camilla Gray, *The Russian Experiment in Art, 1863–1922* (1962), pp. 136–7.
13 Marianne W. Martin, *Futurist Art and Theory* (1968), p. 43. Marinetti's painting, and those of Russolo and Severini discussed later in the chapter, are reproduced in this book.
14 A. C. Birnholz, 'On the Meaning of Kazimir Malevich's "White on White"', *Art International*, XXI no. 1 (1977).
15 Ellen B. Johnson, *Modern Art and the Object* (1976), p. 132.
16 *Ibid.*, p. 113.
17 Many of the du Maurier drawings discussed in this chapter are reproduced in L. Ormond, *George du Maurier* (1969).
18 G. Perry and A. Aldridge, *The Penguin Book of Comics* (1971), p. 161.
19 R. Jenkins, *Essays and Speeches* (1967), p. 232.
20 D. Lloyd George, *Better Times* (1910), pp. 60–144.
21 *Ibid.*, pp. 180–5; *The Great Conspiracy* (1918), p. 157.
22 This chapter is greatly indebted to Eric Partridge's great *Dictionary of Slang and Unconventional English* (fifth edition, 1961), and its *Supplements* down to 1970; glosses, dates, etc., appearing here are from that work unless otherwise noted.
23 K. Horney, *New Ways in Psychoanalysis* (1939), p. 252.

24 H. A. Murray, *Explorations in Personality* (1938) pp. 20–21.
25 R. F. Bales, *Personality and Interpersonal Behaviour* (1970).
26 *Ibid.*, p. 177.
27 *Ibid.*, p. 112; p. 116.
28 A. Inkeles, E. Hanfmann, H. Beier in *Personalities and Cultures*, ed. R. Hunt (1967), pp. 312–39.
29 *Ibid.*, p. 324.
30 Cf. Dante, *Inferno*, XVI. 118–20:

> Ahi quanto cauti uomini esser denno
> presso a color che non veggon pur l'ovra
> ma per entro i pensier miran col senno!
> (Ah how cautious men ought to be, near those who
> do not see merely what is done, but by their insight
> see the thoughts that go on within!)

31 M. Arnold, 'Count Leo Tolstoi', *Essays in Criticism*, second series.
32 For the quotations from Newman see *The Scope and Nature of University Education* (1859 edition), Discourses IV and V.
33 H. T. Odum, *Environment, Power and Society* (1971).
34 G. Snyder, 'The politics of Ethnopoetics', *The Old Ways* (1977), p. 29.
35 *Ibid.*, p. 17.
36 *Earth House Hold* (English edition, 1970), p. 115.
37 *Ibid.*, p. 39 ('Japan First Time Round').
38 *Ibid.*, pp. 121–2.
39 'Hunting, 7': from 'Myths and Texts', in *A Range of Poems* (1966), p. 65.
40 *Ibid.*, p. 53.
41 *Ibid.*, p. 121.
42 *Six Sections from 'Mountains and Rivers without end'* (1964), p. 11.
43 *Ibid.*, p. 28.
44 *Ibid.*, p. 46.
45 *Turtle Island* (1974), p. 58.
46 *The Back Country* (1967 edition), p. 13.
47 *Ibid.*, p. 84.
48 *Earth House Hold*, p. 35.
49 *Ibid.*, p. 120.
50 *The Old Ways*, p. 42.
51 *Earth House Hold*, p. 4.
52 *A Range of Poems*, p. 117.
53 *Mountains and Rivers*, p. 34
54 *Turtle Island*, pp. 82–3.
55 Howitt, *Native Tribes*, p. 275.

56 R. M. Berndt, *Love Songs of Arnhem Land* (1978).

57 *Ibid.*, p. 229.

58 *Ibid.*, pp. 227–8.

59 Slightly adapted from W. W. Trask, *The Unwritten Song* (1969), pt I, p. 242; quoted there from Catherine H. Berndt, 'Expressions of grief among aboriginal women', *Oceania*, xx (1949–50), p. 303.

60 Reproduced in G. Dutton, *Russell Drysdale* (1964).

61 Quotations in this chapter are from Muir's *Collected Poems* (1960); from the second edition of *Self Condemned* (1954); and from the Penguin editions of *Wolf Solent* and *The Eye of the Storm*.

62 M. Lowry, *Letters* (1967), p. 80.